THE TROU
PARALLEL UNIVERSES

NEW WRITING FROM ROEHAMPTON

Edited by
Leone Ross

FINCHAM PRESS

First published 2014
Published by Fincham Press
        University of Roehampton
        Department of English and Creative Writing
        80 Roehampton Lane
        London SW15 5PH, UK

Design by Rudolf Ammann
Typeset in Calluna and Calluna Sans
Printed and bound by printondemand-worldwide.com
Printed in England

British Library Cataloguing in Publication Data
A catalogue record for this book is available from
the British Library.

ISBN 978-0-9928581-0-0

1. Creative writing; 2. University press; 3. Fiction; 4. Poetry;
5. Nonfiction; 6. Illustration

CONTENTS

FOREWORD

In April 2013, at the London Book Fair, Fincham Press made its first public appearance. Speaking alongside fellow panellists from University College London (UCL), we pointed to a new wave of innovation in publishing that was taking place in British universities – the site of an earlier revolution centuries earlier, when the book first travelled from the religious to the secular realm.

Fincham Press, now putting its first title out into the world, represents an attempt to put those ideas into practice and add innovation in *form* and *process* to the experiments in *content* that already occupy so much of our teaching life.

It also offers a new way for us to serve our students, past and present. This first title is a student anthology; other strands on the publishing list will focus on other things such as pedagogy, essays, creative and scholarly work. But the way in which we, as publishers, can help their work find a public will add another dimension to what is already on offer, just as the contribution made by the students enriches the publisher and its host, the Department of English and Creative Writing at the University of Roehampton.

A big thanks from the three of us, the founding editorial board, to all those who helped make this publishing launch possible. Special thanks is due to Rudolf Ammann, Jeff Hillson, Peter Jaeger, Laura Peters and James Smythe.

Susan Greenberg
Leone Ross
Louise Tondeur

INTRODUCTION
By Leone Ross

Writers live in parallel universes.

That's the trouble, sometimes – the perpetual call of alternate reality. We are tempted by the infinite options available in a moment's concentration: one good idea and we're in a whole different world, equipped with erudite wit or the capacity to inspire the masses, peopled by better lovers and friends. Another universe, where we control the rhythm and vocabulary in a poem's stanza, where the very nature of meaning is at our fingertips. Most people have experienced *l'esprit de l'escalier* or staircase wit, the dilemma of thinking of the perfect retort too late. If you're a writer, you can use that zinger in the next poem or screenplay. You can place that perfect phrase in greyed-out type; make polar bears into poetry; even re-cast the work of the writers you admire.

All that and more happens in the pages of this book.

The physical act of writing can also feel like inhabiting an alternate universe. After a writing session in which he has attained near-complete immersion, the writer emerges blinking, feeling that he has been somewhere else. This state of energised focus was dubbed 'the flow' by Hungarian psychologist Mihály Csíkszentmihályi, who says that its characteristics include distorted temporal experience. Creative practice changes one's subjective experience of time.

Dr Melanie C. Green, psychologist at the University of North Carolina, studies the effects of story narrative on human behaviour. In an interview on David McNeary's regular podcast 'You're Not So Smart', Green says the urge to storytell may derive from a human need to practice connecting past and future – a key ability that enables us to predict likely future events. For example, a woman who nearly freezes to death in the winter needs to remember that experience and plan a strategy to survive subsequent winters. If she cannot, she risks death. Storytelling may be a safe way to practice this skill, surfing imaginary universes without risking actual dangerous events.

Writers who have not yet been published dream of a parallel universe in which their work is enjoyed by as many people as possible. For most of the writers here, this is their first experience of publication; certainly in trade paperback. Each of the 28 pieces – poetry, fiction and creative nonfiction – were entered into an annual Creative Writing Day Anthology competition run by the Department of English and Creative Writing at the University of Roehampton. Creative Writing Day began in 2006, spearheaded by Dr Louise Tondeur as a day of events to promote the undergraduate and postgraduate writing programmes, and to celebrate writers and writing.

In Spring 2008, we began a competition, publishing winners in our online magazine *Roehampton Writes*, edited by Dr Susan Greenberg. Creative Writing Day has become a key university calendar event and a learning opportunity for our students. A student volunteer team plans the annual soirée where competition winners read to an audience that includes editors, agents, published writers, and Roehampton alumni who now work in the business. Volunteers develop skills in arts organisation, leadership, negotiation, event hosting and editorial assessment. They plan and host the event and form an editorial board that long-lists the competition entries, before staff complete the shortlist and announce the winners. Staff judges have included poets Dr Peter Jaeger and Jeff Hilson, and novelists Dr James Smythe and Dr Louise Tondeur.

When the department began in earnest to plan an imprint of its own, in 2013, it seemed obvious to begin by publishing winners of the latest competition: the material was ready to go and publishing our students is our pleasure. Even better to celebrate the new press with a special, bumper edition that puts the most recent winners alongside earlier favourites. Fourteen of our final 28 writers are previous winners of the Creative Writing Day competition.

If the central concept of parallel universes is an infinite number of paths and choices, this is the one where these particular writers publish in the company of each other. So what is here, in this particular mash-up?

The first writer selected from past competitors was Tom Watts. Winner of the Editor's Choice award in 2008 and 2009, his short story 'The Sea and the Shore' has, he modestly agreed, stood the test of time. What distinguishes Watts's writing is his clear empathy for characters so different from him. The sea and the shore are characters too: captured with the lightest of strokes.

Harry Godwin's 'Polar Bear Sequence 3' was chosen next: its relaxed wit appealed and its inclusion provides evidence of the programme's commitment to innovative poetry and texts of all kinds. Michael Zand's 'The Lexico Project' manages to be a poem, an experiment in politics and linguistics and very funny to boot, recalling pleasant memories of Zand's dry, witty reading on Creative Writing Day 2009. The experiment continued with Rebecca Rosier's 'Whistling Through Teeth & Eating Chocolate Orange', a piece that seemed to meet and kiss at the moment between pleasure and pain; of relationships lost and the self wrestled back to safety. Diana Nortey's 'Boys and Girlfriends', a tiny ode to young boys in cities and their worries about girls, was a 'found' piece of art. Part eavesdrop, part edit, it is a testimony to an urban slang found nowhere but London town.

The year 2012 was a good one for these young writers. Amy Austen's capacity for sheer joy meant that she had to open this collection, and her memoir 'Tick-Tock' provides a snapshot of unabashed British exuberance. Lewis Spratt's narrative poem 'Fairground Kaleidoscope' is a suitably odd and deliberately accessible introduction to our poetry selection, walking that fine line between play, seduction and poignancy. 'Kaleidoscope' sat well between the memoried world of Austen and Jack Charter's 'Wide Open', a wonderfully restrained take on fathering, power struggles and OCD. Louise Young's 'Lunar Effect' was delivered, at that year's soirée, with the appropriate measure of swag and Geordie accent and is a great exemplar of the word play nurtured by our writing programme. The same is true of Hedda Estensen's magnificent re-write of ee cummings's 'My Girl's Lofty With Tall Dark Eyes'. Apart from its unapologetic declaration of female sensuality, Estensen's title (page 41) is the most fun in the collection.

Nicholas Elliott's 'The End of a Pier' is a dark story of a marriage gone very wrong indeed. Combining the existential angst of a twenty-something with an older world-weary despair, Elliott creates an anti-hero who will inspire recognition and dislike in equal measure. Toni Dipple's delicate, fragile 'movements', plucked from a longer work, '39 Measures of Absence', is full of longing, sensuality, mourning and accountability. Rounding off that year's crop of winners is Steph Vickers, plumbing her childhood to commit 'Hark The Herald Angel' to paper. Winner of the 2012 Editor's Choice, Vickers's frank but gentle portrayal of a little girl struggling with Christmas is testament to the old adage, less is more.

The winning entries of 2013 make up most of this anthology. Moving between science fiction and horror fiction, magic realism and intertextuality, the 2013 cohort begins with second-time winner Emma Strand and her short story, 'Letters to Martha'. An apocalyptic love story with shades of Angela Carter, it was a favourite with the student board and staff judges alike. A fine successor to Estensen's word play is Haley Jenkins's 'Lachrymose'. While a poem of completely different timbre, form and mood, 'Lachrymose' nevertheless stands in a fine tradition of exaggeration and sense made non-sense – especially when one's theme is writing itself. 'Semiprecious Flarfers offset socialism', indeed.

The Trouble With Parallel Universes references the globe, from Thailand to Spain and the Arctic. MA student Amanda Frieze's 'Dusty Magazine' is the competition's first-ever novel excerpt, set in America. An uncompromising look at poverty and the first stirrings of sexuality, it leaves us feeling a different kind of desolate to Bill Carey's 'Sleepless', also set in the USA; a chilling examination of fame and all that it brings with it. Emily Parsons's 'Flathead' and Jo Schinas's 'The Rabbit' make for another interesting pair. While these two writers possess entirely distinctive voices, they share a similar capacity for tenderness and subtlety. The deaths their characters witness, while also different, echo long after the book is closed, leaving the same taste of sadness.

Audrey Jean's small, stellar poem, 'we met in outer soundscape', winds across the page, whispering ambition. It benefits from being in the same collection as the tender, erotic spell cast by the female protagonist in Madeleine Morris's 'Fixed in Amber'. Both pieces are wonderful examples of Jean's 'terrible nothing' and the power of the female gaze. Think of Morris's work as the longer, prose version of Jean's poem – and the latter as the kind of incantation spoken by Morris's protagonist if we could just hear her in the moment of climax. Spells and game-changing female protagonists abound in this book, with Emma Riddell's small but perfectly formed feminist horror story, 'The Plague Poppet' leaving behind just the kind of shiver that good horror should. What kind of parallel universe did Heidi Larsen explore to find her intertextually woven, biblical 'Sectioned'? In a category of its own, this surrealist rambling explores a mind truly on the brink of everything: hell, ecstacy, redemption, terror, love. Sean Wai Keung's dreams of poisoned marmalade in 'A Different Light' return us to quintessential Englishness and together with Sandra Williamson's 'Such Is Life', calls upon memory and loss to explore the detail of family, the ties that bind and the art of homage. Nanou Blair Gould's convincing magical realist tale, 'My Lady of Shalott', literally coaxes art to step out into the world and offer love as an antidote to a questionable childhood. Gould reminds us it is not easy to raise children who are aware of alternative realities.

The penultimate tale, Peter Benney's titular 'The Trouble With Parallel Universes' offers the kind of dark humour deserving of kudos; an evocative story of a haunted essay-writer, it reiterates the infinite nature of possibility and the importance of choice and perception.

The final word is claimed, not merely granted. Katie Seth's 'The Write Thing' is a funny, scathingly feisty examination of the creative writing process that should be required reading for first-year students. It offers a final flourish of mischievous joy.

Writers and editors meet in yet another kind of parallel universe: a murky, complex, hard-working space, where the writer – with support – seeks to crystallise focus and creative intention.

What comes of it all is an object, a *thing*; hopefully a beautiful thing, or a thing of integrity, arresting or true: ultimately fit for public consumption. The writer holds this object between his hands, this thing made of words – and worlds collide: intention, aesthetic, memory, confessed secrets and lies, metaphor, wishes, fears.

And so we peer into each other's worlds.

TICK-TOCK

By Amy Austen

We spend half the weekend standing around in the back-yard, with the sunshine and the ferret and the ticks. Fascinated by the never-ending supply of the creatures, we purchase a tiny, green device, specially designed, and spend hours unscrewing the ticks from the ferret's flesh. Each parasite is examined with delighted horror and transferred to a jar full of alcohol, where we hope they will die in a drunken stupor.

Drink of the moment is Pimm's, with lemonade and a selection of fruit. A new drink for me, I find it refreshing and innocent; am particularly amused by the addition of cucumber later in the day. It slides down my throat, grated silk, and flavours my tongue so the air tastes sweet.

I mix up fairy cakes, and decorate them with icing and cherries and people love them. I make dozens but they don't last long; everyone is too happy to think about diets. The atmosphere is warm laziness; my brothers lounge in peeling deck chairs, shirts over their shoulders. The sky is an intense blue with unreachable clouds; beneath my feet the toasty bricks burn red in contrast.

We settle into the halcyon feel of the day. Those too squeamish to look at the ticks make bets on how many, in total, we will pull off the ferret. Our highest guess is not even half right. The jar spins with blood and wriggling black legs. The hairs on my forearm ripple vertically. Laughter explodes between the old walls; different accents mix under the blue umbrella.

The ferret gets restless and shadows shrink back under the table. We box up flapjacks and head out into the humming streets. Blues music finds us on the sea breeze. Senhouse Street is happy and crowded, spotted with flip-flops and ice cream, and we twist through the bodies and end up at the Calor Gas stage, where the road slopes gently into the quay and the Solway Firth is a watercolour haze in the distance. We settle into the hot crunchy tarmac; there's a certain novelty in being able to sit cross-legged in the heart of the road. Pints are perched between thighs, empties lining the pavement and railings.

Roll up your jeans; it's officially summertime and you've got the best seats in town.

Classic riffs charge the still air, salty with the sea and the smell of fish and chips. A dedicated mob bounce about by the band and their crazy laughter gurgles above the hum of the tarmac crowd. We are up and dancing now, barefoot in the street, and it feels like I'm dreaming this strange reality, where I belong. We are family: together; a sphere of grinning faces, flashing with sunlight, twirling in the madness.

FAIRGROUND KALEIDOSCOPE

By Lewis Spratt

Look
through
a
fairground
kaleidoscope –
there's
nothing
in there
dude,
there's
nothing
in
there.

Her hair was red and nails blue and yellow tipped. She drank cold Coke and I felt guilty for adding rum to mine. I asked her what the flowers on her dress were and what she called the colour of her lipstick; she wasn't sure and pointed to the flashing lights of the Waltzer. We have to go on the Waltzer. But the Teacups may be fun, plus we could talk. We have to go on the Waltzer. It's about the same time the guy spins us faster that I realise I don't know her age. I don't know if I'm drunk or the spinning is making me drunk. I hear a rifle shot and a bell ringing and a clown shouting at a child and I don't know her age or why she holds the rum. I squint my eyes at the pink pounding light and turn to her and see it in her eyes. She's pulled up her jumper and there's a tattoo of a lady on her lower arm, perhaps a gypsy, crying pearl-shaped tears. She's trying to tug me towards the Haunted House but I don't want to go. I take her behind the burger stand and she thinks I want to kiss her. I want to know why she's crying. Why is she crying? Because it's pretty she tells me. Don't you think it's pretty?

WIDE OPEN

By Jack Charter

Dad was a private man. He worked as an assistant at a bank, standing behind a desk, telling customers about different money plans. One day, his boss came round for dinner.

We lived in an expensive detached house on the outskirts of London, with fake wooden beams around the windows and potted plants flanking the porch. The boss came at six o'clock, knocking at the front door. All of our family friends knew not to use the front one. Dad didn't like it: the thought of opening it to the street made him shiver; like someone stepped on his grave, he told me. Even the Indian takeaway knew not to use it, and the postman.

I heard Dad coming down the stairs, and watched from the kitchen with a glass of water as he walked into the hall. When he got to the front door he crouched on the doormat, his polo shirt tightening around the bump of his spine. He lifted the metal letter-flap, and moved his head towards it.

'Use the back door if you could, Mr Johnson,' he said, holding up the flap. I couldn't hear Mr Johnson's reply. 'Through the fence on the right – it's unlocked,' Dad continued, 'then through the back door, sir.'

I took a sip of cold water and leant against the kitchen surface. The bland, savoury smell of chicken wafted from the steamer. Dad jogged down the hall, and into the kitchen.

'Out the way a minute,' he said to me. 'Johnson's arrived.' He went and stood at the back door; a pane of glass with a plastic frame, through which late orange daylight shone. He puffed out his chest and straightened his back. He rolled his shoulders, once, twice. Then he put his arms out in front of him, and rested his hands one on top of the other, on his pelvis, to look presentable. The door handle clicked, and I felt a rush of cool air from outside.

'Come in, sir. I'm sorry about having to go round the –' Dad stopped, and leant forward slightly. 'Is everything alright?' he asked.

Mr Johnson moved past him, into the light of the room. His face was covered in fake tan, as orange as the light outside. There was a terrier-sized paw print on his trouser leg.

'Your dog attacked me in the garden,' he said.

Dad looked down at the tiny stain on his boss's trousers, closed his mouth and swallowed. 'I apologise – she can be a nuisance with strangers. I'll get you a sponge right away –'

'No, no.' Mr Johnson shook his head slowly, as if he'd suffered a great injury, and as he moved his head from side to side, his dark neck hairs swept the top of his collar. 'Just a glass of water, please.'

Dad, Mr Johnson and I sat at the living room table. The wood stove burned under the mantelpiece. A shade of red mixed with the orange of Mr Johnson's face, brought out by the heat of the room. On each of our plates were steamed chicken cubes, peas, carrots, and half a jacket potato on the side. None of it was seasoned. Dad's cooking never was.

'Now, Mr Grahams,' Mr Johnson said, chewing one of the chicken cubes and swallowing. 'Let's revise our goals for the new quarter.'

Dad looked up from his plate, nodding eagerly.

Mr Johnson rushed through a list, full of financial slang. He spoke as if he'd gone over it with their employees dozens of times before, and was bored of the whole thing. When he finished, he looked around the room, perhaps annoyed my father hadn't added much to his list of stale ideas. Then he noticed an old map above the mantelpiece, with a couple of pins sticking out of it.

'What's that, Mr Grahams? A map of Africa?' He leaned back in his chair.

Dad nodded. 'My wife's been there a month now.'

'Really? Strange place for a holiday.'

'Oh no, not a holiday.' Dad perked up, as if Mr Johnson would find this subject particularly interesting. He put the sides of his palms flat on the table, with a distance between them. 'She's doing charity work, starting in Morocco. Then she's off again in a couple of months, working her way down the continent.'

Mr Johnson didn't say anything. He was staring at a potted areca palm in the corner of the room.

'That plant needs watering,' he said indignantly, as if it'd been too long since he'd last spoken. 'Don't you think?'

He got up from his seat at the table and went over to the plant, taking his glass of water with him. He began whistling, and ran one of his big hands across the leaves. They were dry and yellowed, almost dead. One floated down to the carpet and landed next to his polished shoe. He looked at it, shrugged his shoulders, and tipped what was left of his water – about half the glass – into the plant pot from a standing height. Some of it splashed up from the earth and soaked into the carpet. Mr Johnson didn't seem to notice.

'Let's give it some light as well,' he said. It was late evening, but the orange glow still illuminated the closed curtains. He went to open them, when Dad yelled out:

'No.'

Mr Johnson turned around, one hand still poised on the curtain. His mouth hung open at the sound of the voice, suddenly loud and authoritative.

'I apologise,' Dad said. 'But I like to keep them closed.' I noticed that his lips were quivering slightly.

Mr Johnson lowered his hand and let it fall to his side. He turned, walked back to the table, and sat down.

'I see,' he said, blinking hard, as if he'd never heard a more impertinent outburst. I saw his eyelids were a pale pink, where he'd forgotten to apply the tan. He drummed his fingers on the table.

'So...how's your wife funding this African venture?' he said. 'It sounds rather expensive.'

'It is,' Dad replied, still breathing hard. 'Especially as she won't be working for a while. It's all coming out of my pocket.'

'I see. The money's coming from your job at my bank,' Mr Johnson said, his eyes wide. In the places where his dark hair was thinning, his scalp shone with sweat. Dad looked at me, obviously wanting to excuse me from the table, but Mr Johnson spoke again.

'Because – and let me be blunt here, Mr Grahams – by all accounts, you're a rather idle employee. You stand behind your desk, chatting idly with customers, without selling any of the plans you've been asked to.' He leaned back in his chair once again, his hairy stomach visible in an opening between two shirt buttons.

Dad opened and closed his mouth a couple of times, taking in small gasps of air. 'Let me tell you, sir, that's the first time I've heard anything against myself as an employee. I am honest, yes; I am honest. If a customer can't find a plan that suits them, I'll –'

'Tell them to go to another bank, Mr Grahams? That's not why you earn your salary. That's not why you can afford this nice big house, and your wife's ventures in Africa.'

'Charity work, Mr Johnson, my wife's doing –'

'Yes, your nice big house,' Mr Johnson interrupted. 'Which can't be entered without being attacked by a *dog*.' He breathed in deeply through his nostrils. A few painful moments passed. Dad simply looked down at the table, his eyes glazed. Everyone could tell there was nothing left to say.

'Now, Mr Grahams, I'll be leaving.' Mr Johnson picked up his briefcase from beside the table leg, folded his jacket over his arm, and walked out to the hall.

'Use the back door, please,' Dad called after him. But he had turned right, towards the front door. 'The back door,'

Dad repeated, but he didn't seem to hear. Dad rose from his seat and walked out of the living room. Watching from the table, I saw Mr Johnson, frozen next to the front door, his orange hand clasping the doorknob. Dad put a shaking hand on his shoulder, but Mr Johnson turned slowly and brushed it away, his big chest raising and lowering. Under his combed parting his small black eyes shone, receding in their sockets. His thin lips curled into a grin, showing small, sharp teeth.

'Mr Grahams, I'd like to exit by this door. If you won't allow me to, it'll cost you your job.'

Dad looked back at me, his brow creased and heavy: this wasn't something he wanted me to hear. Mr Johnson didn't move, his chest still rising and falling steadily. He drew in his lower lip, and slid the tip of his tongue across it, left to right.

Dad arched forward, looking down at his socks.

'Can't do it,' he murmured. He was shaking. He said it louder. 'I *can't* do it.'

Dad lost his job, and sold the house soon after. Mum had to cut short her stay in Morocco, and she hasn't been to Africa since. We don't have the money. We moved into a two bedroom flat, and Mum began to stay in her room a lot of the time. I don't think she ever really forgave him.

Dad and I visited the old house recently. Mum didn't want to come along – didn't want to see what the new people had done to it.

As we came up to the house, I rolled down the car window and looked out. The windows on either side of the porch were open, with the curtains drawn back, letting in the white light of day. The front door was wide open too, and I could see all the way through the house: all the way down the hall, to the sink glinting in the kitchen. Everything was lit by the sun, and there were two young brown-skinned girls with braids playing on the patio outside, laughing. The potted ferns in the windows were green and alive, and the smell of spices wafted in through my window.

Still, Dad didn't look. He stared forward, thinking his own private thoughts, concentrating on the road.

LETTERS TO MARTHA

By Emma Strand

First Letter

M,

My right arm is squeaking again.

I wish I could open our letters just once by asking how you are. How are you? I'm afraid that sounds awfully insincere.

I'm far too sentimental today. This arm is starting to rust; yet, as ever, Dr. Epsilon slicks the oil from his grease-ridden head to his hand and fiddles with my gears before telling me, 'It's all to be expected'. He never quite manages to let slip exactly what's to be expected, only that I should be expecting it. It is as a train that never comes.

Sometimes I think the real sickness exists in those left behind; ergo, it exists in me. Epsilon was more machine than man, even before this began. Now he administers prescriptions of cogs and keys to almost all who visit him. He hails himself Horologist, Surgeon and Emperor of All Things Newfangled in New England the Eighth.

He's converted all of the churches to factories. Those who will not submit to his 'enhancements' enter through the heavy wooden doors and kneel at the altar of his insanity. They become cogs and keys one way or another. Disappearing in plumes of violet smoke above the steeples.

My arm had the sickness, that's what he told me; that's why he hacked it off and fixed me up with my current languid limb. I was lucky. Perhaps he still has my bones, somewhere? Perhaps he intends to bury them so that the people of the future can excavate and excuse my very existence.

My arm aches with the burden of tomorrow, and what it may bring.

Unless of course, it brings you.

Always, Atticus.

Second Letter

'I could be bounded in a nutshell, and count myself a king of infinite space, were it not that I have bad dreams.'

You always liked *Hamlet*.

Someone once told me that if you wake a person having a nightmare they are more likely to remember it; but if you let them sleep, if you let them suffer, they are more likely to forget it. So, I wonder: which is kinder?

Always, Atticus.

Third Letter

Epsilon has fashioned clockwork bees so that he may proceed to pollinate tin can plants. He says that someday there may be summer again. A stopped clock is right twice daily, and yet, otherwise idle like an arrow-less compass.

I should have saved you.

The clockwork bees buzz when their miniature metal bodies get too close to your ears. This is his attention to detail. At least two of them have run out of wind and fallen from flight in the time it has taken to write you this letter. He's made far too many. I want to crush them, but they are too special, too much of a work of art to be busted by the boot. Epsilon wouldn't have it. Then again, how would he know? I bet he counts them, Scrooge counting his coins.

Are you where I left you: buried in the garden, gnawed at by the sickness, alone?

Wait for me, I will be with you.
Sleep softly,
Always, Atticus.

Fourth Letter

M,

It's been a while since my last confession.

By candlelight, in this broken building, I have been burning for a cigarette. The last empty pouch of Amber Leaf tobacco I had in my possession has lost its allure. It has surrendered its scent to the thickness of the air and dispersed like the pathogens of a slow motion sneeze. Do you remember when cancer was the sickness? Then this usurper stole away its crown of thorns.

The Sickness had no name, no vaccine, and no mercy. Only a select few could fight it off. The first sign was the loosening and losing of teeth. Then, slowly, slowly it turned the blood solid, like snake venom. Why us? I lost so much more than just my arm when the sepsis, the psychosis, the gangrene set in.

Before, there were cigarettes. There may not have been much else. But at least there were cigarettes.

I went back to see Epsilon. He fixed me, begrudgingly, seeing it as more of an opportunity to brag about his newest designs than to genuinely enquire about my wellbeing. Why should he? My index and middle finger joints had seized entirely. Erect in their Victory England stance, it was almost impossible to stretch a glove over them in order to go outside. I wear the glove for two reasons; firstly to disguise my 'enhancement' from the eyes of those survivors deemed unworthy of Epsilon's efforts. I see them in the streets, stalking those with gleaming attachments. They are the beggars and shadows of our new world, scavengers ready to trade their snatched fragments of metal on the black market. Here in

New England the Eighth we know nothing of what goes on beyond the borders of our isolated island. Or so we say; if you talk to the right people at the right time of night they can smuggle a whisper in a wishing jar over the seas.

Metal is currency; attachments are the only antidote to the sickness. To paraphrase Epsilon, 'copper cannot catch the common cold!' He's telling the truth: I will not shrivel up or rot. I will rust, perhaps, as I know all too well. That's another reason for the glove; attachments have a tendency to go green in the rain. Epsilon says the upgrades will be much more enduring.

Those unenhanced survivors also have mouths to feed. They spend their time breeding because they have nothing better to do. They relish the human leftovers from a good scavenge. There was a rumour that Epsilon controlled an Animal Farm in the New England the Eighth North, but you can't trust rumours from people who eat people. It does something to them: turns them into empty shells. It backs them into corners that they can't escape from.

I'm sorry. I don't mean to frighten you. I am quite safe. I stay useful to Epsilon in order to stay alive. When I am not writing to you, I write for him, as scholar and scribe. I can't say anything more in case these letters are intercepted. I have already said too much. I just don't know how I am sup-posed to type with one hand!

Always, Atticus.

Fifth Letter

M,

It snowed! Yesterday, for the first time in the history of the future! The dirt on the ground quickly turned it to brown slush, but, for a moment, as I stood at the window watching the flurry fall from the sky, there was hope.

I had another dream; of you, in fickle fondness. In our old world, our old lives, abandoned yet intact in my mind.

As is our love. As are we.

If you dropped and smashed my love, it would not make it lost. What remains in the jagged sharpness is the softness of my love. From there its roots cannot be pulled. Would you recognise my love, if you saw it on the street, begging for change, shoeless, hopeless? Far from the clouds from which it formed? In my days you cease to be, but in my dreams you sing.

Always, Atticus.

Sixth Letter

M,
Welcome to a world of Low Tech and High Life, not meant for us.

I buried you in the garden because I couldn't bear to lose you. When I heard your key in the front door, I knew. I saw your mouth, congealed blood at the corners of your lips and your two front teeth shaking in your palm. Wet streaks down your face. The Sickness had set in. I was certain. If death did not come for you the police would, there was no choice, no time. I'd planned to hang myself after I buried you, you didn't deserve the indignity of not being buried. I wanted to give you that. But you couldn't go through with it. I clamped my hands over your face, too tightly. Too long. You struggled, weakened in my arms. It was the only way. Please.

If only I had not wasted all that time digging. Then I could be where I should be, cold in the ground with you. I caught the Sickness from you and then they came for me. I told them you escaped New England, a lie they freely believed, yet now you'll never leave.

There is no silence like your silence.

I am going to give these letters to Epsilon. I am going to make amends.

Answer me this? Do you dream of me, as I am, as I was, or as I will be?

Always, Atticus.

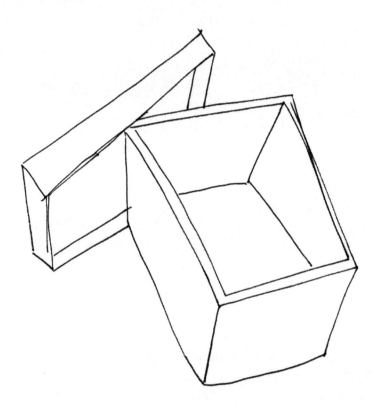

Wanted to Empty Box 2 (Tamar Levi)

39 MEASURES OF ABSENCE
[EXTRACT]

By Toni Dipple

A woman sits on
the corner of
their bed;
looking[1]

[1] (at what remains)

On her grey desk
sleeps the ashtray
he used
often[2]

She holds her breasts:
his fingerprints' echo
dusts her
skin[3]

[3] (with brandy, tobacco, earth and ink, coffee and cum and bread)

His blue pen rests
on paper made
heavy with
thoughts[4]

A breeze moves through
the open sash
turning unexamined
lines[5]

[5] (although beautiful and precise, his words were not always complimentary)

She rolls a cigarette
and smokes by
the unclothed
window[6]

[6] (a flame born of oil and flint and kept alive by breath)

LUNAR EFFECT

By Louise Young

Lashing out
Cashing in
Spoils the grinning things.
Corners coined by
Wrecks.
Wrecks already barely twenty. Shot
from shackles of style and bottles of bile
Mildly frightening for insiders, dare-dream.
Dare
Just stare out. Only cry out
On a night out.
Sparkles of sorrow seize the scene
To bleach a bass line with a scary-eyed screech!
And smart like dirty smirks.
It's a familiar gown – worn
in a bilious town
Good binge, bad binge we all fall down.

In this postcard from the most hard there's
spiders in glitter and garters
with tigers in denim and daughters.
If you want to feel the force before body and soul divorce
you follow them.
An absent green fairy's a bastard green giant,
a vicious spore.
Talk backwards this drink, faster, more
Neck. Snap. Back
Open, Smile
Pour.

Politely
When the hub of all the squalor wears the bodies like a collar
It's only unsightly, slightly
Now you're feeling it nicely.
Down dicing dark
Smoked in soak
A fiver floats
in garlic sauce and saliva.
We're higher not mightier.
All grown up and buying a bed
The head wants a treble when the trouble's never dead
now she's back from the rubble and she struggles with her
legs.
Heels stab cold in cobbles,
and she finds a little tipple incites a little topple

And you know that she'll break, but she's fine with the
brink.
She'd tell you herself but she's telling a drink.
Up in a blue light
Up in a cat fight
Not up in the morning
Coaxing, calling
A reductive spawn.
A seductive storm.
Slipping neons in your drip
and every door's a dawn
gating a fantastic crash.
And every door's a date
gating a drowning.
And every door framed with bench-pressed funeral squaddies
Depressed benchmark Blighty
winks,
in cosy formality
and tells you to mind the gravity.

BOYS AND GIRLFRIENDS

By Diana Nortey

They are talking to each other, walking side by side in the early March afternoon. The first friend is pale as a piece of paper and the other friend is brown, like caramel. The train station is damp from the Spring rain. They both sit down on a metal seat with the white paint chipping off. It's 12:50, and their train is due at one.

'Anorexic woman!'

'Shut up!'

'You're a waste, man, you're a dickhead, you're a pussy!'

'What are you talking about?'

'You and this skinny-ass girlfriend you used to be with.'

'Why you gonna go and diss her like that? Why you calling me a pussy for? I've told you this a thousand times. She had some sort of disorder and anything she would eat, she wouldn't put on weight. She just used to smoke. Bare cigarettes.' The pale-coloured friend leans on the metal seat, looking at the other boy playing on a portable game player.

'I was worried about her. But I was with her innit, it's not like you're gonna be with someone and just let them do what they're doing.'

He looks his friend dead in the eyes.

'What, man?'

'You know she looked good. My girl. Even though she was skinny yeah, she still had long brown hair, big hazel eyes, legs that hypnotized me into a daze, and the skinniest fingers that gave me a hard-on.'

'Look at you tryna buss out some lyrics! She ain't even your girl no more.' The caramel-skinned boy looks back at his game player. 'OK, for real though, I'll stop making fun about your girl. Ex-girl. I had a girlfriend who used to drink though. Seriously like, her parents had some drinking problems. They went to the pub every *day*, bruv! Every day! Drinking lagers, ciders and other shit. I don't even drink that much, like! But bwoy, she came to see me pissed out of her face, wanting to shag me, bad! Man...

'What?'

'Nah nah, it's nothing. But she got serious problems though. There's even too much to say, like... bwoy.'

'Are you guys still together?'

'More like on a break, bruv. We still talk and what-not, but it's not the same, like.'

'It couldn't be as bad as mine, at least you're still talking to your girl.'

'True, but still. I hope she hasn't caught nothing.'

'From what?'

'Nah, I dunno like, she's drinking all the time innit, so like she don't remember a lot of things. Like the other week, it was her birthday! How you gonna forget your birthday?'

'Ha, not me!'

'Exactly like, that's how bad it's gotten so I dunno if I should leave her, or stay with her. I don't wanna change her because bwoy, she has a temper as well.'

'I bet my girl could beat your girl *any* day.'

'Pssh! Don't be stupid now bruv, your girl was some stick.'

'Whatever man, she can beat your girl's ass!'

'Bruv. Shut your mouth.'

'So now you know how it feels when someone is trash talking someone you love, yeah?'

'Bruv, why you being all mushy for?'

'What? You don't like talking about your girlfriend now?'

'Didn't say that, did I? Why we talkin' about this anyways, we gonna link some chicks?'

'No, you're going to link some chicks, you just want me

to come along.'

The announcement for the 1pm train blares through the speakers. They both get on the train, looking at two skinny girls with long blonde hair.

DUSTY MAGAZINE
[EXTRACT FROM A NOVEL]

By Amanda Frieze

Mom always kicked me out of the house in the summer when there wasn't school. 'Go play, and don't come back until supper,' she'd say, then slam the screen door behind me. Me and my bud Johnny would play outside and cause trouble from sunup to sundown. We were best buds, me and Johnny, but we couldn't have looked more different. I was kind of a short kid, and I was white, really pale, you know? Except when I was sunburnt, and then I was red. But Johnny was tall and black. So black he looked blue sometimes if the sun was hitting him right.

He lived up the street with his parents – who were both blind – and his younger twin brothers. His family was even poorer than me and Mom, living off disability benefits and such, so Johnny did lots of stuff around the house. One day I went over there and he was cutting his kid brother's hair. Another time he was helping his Dad fix a door handle. Imagine that, ten years old and doing all that grown-up stuff!

Johnny was brave too. I remember this one time I went over to his house, and he had a baby boa constrictor wrapped around his neck. 'Christ, that's dangerous,' I said to him. But Johnny said the snake liked him. He took it with him almost everywhere after that.

We lived in the desert, and behind the row of houses on our street was a huge vacant field filled with nothing but dirt and tumbleweeds and this one Joshua tree. The land must have been a couple of acres at least. It got windy out there, which is why the weeds were called tumbleweeds. The dead ones tumbled round and round like wheels when it got windy. There was this spot on the side of the field furthest from our houses where all the tumbleweeds blew and gathered, up against a tall chain link fence that separated the field from a bunch of rich people's houses that all looked the same. Those weeds clung to the fence with their thorns. Layers of them stuck together so tight that eventually they were so thick you couldn't see through them to the other side of the fence.

That's how Johnny and me got the idea to make a tumbleweed fort. We wanted a place to hang out where no one could see us, that felt like it was our own. Before the fort, I didn't feel like I had a place that was mine. Sure, I lived in a house, but it was Mom's house, and everything that happened in it had to be Mom's way. I wanted to feel grown-up and do my own thing, where it didn't matter if I was dirty, and where I wouldn't get bossed around. And I think Johnny needed a place where he could be less like a grown-up. At his house, he always had to be responsible, almost like another parent to his younger brothers, on account of how their real parents couldn't do everything because they were blind. But he was still a kid, you know? And he wanted to do kid things, like set up an aquarium for his snake and collect comic books.

It took us a few days to make the fort. We learned that if you picked up a dead weed from the bottom part of the stem, you wouldn't get poked because there weren't thorns there. We collected tumbleweeds for days from all over the field, and linked them one by one, starting from the weeds already gathered against the chain link fence, and forming a circle all round us. Then we knotted another layer of weeds all around that circle of weeds, so it was double thick. Those weeds were as good as nailed together by the time the thorns got all entangled, and the layers made it so no one could see us when we were standing inside them, except for maybe birds and planes flying overhead.

In the field there were paths carved out by the dirt bikes that the older boys from our neighbourhood had, and we'd ride our bicycles for hours on those tracks when those boys weren't around. Man, but it was hot. On a summer day it could get up to a hundred-ten degrees and we'd be out there sweating, feeling like we were going to die of thirst. The taste in my mouth was salty dust, from the sweat that ran down the side of my face and the mess kicked up by the wind. We had to go back to one of our houses to get water. If we were close to my house, we'd drink from the hose. If we were near Johnny's, his mom would feel around for lemons and ice, and give us cold water with half a lemon in each glass.

We were walking on one of the dirt paths this one hot afternoon in early June, a couple days after we'd finished building the fort, Johnny with his snake round his neck, me with a big stick, whacking at the weeds. We were tired from biking, so we weren't talking. The only sound was the wind, whistling through the air; that, and the whack whack of my stick. I was aiming for tumbleweeds when I saw something out of the corner of my eye. Something bright that didn't match the normal tan and brown colours of the desert.

It was a magazine.

'Lookee here,' I said, breaking the silence. I wrestled it out from the middle of the weed. Those weeds had about a thousand thorns on them and the one covering the magazine scratched my hand so bad it bled.

'What is it?' Johnny asked. I didn't answer. I was just staring at one of the pages, my mouth hanging open. I had never seen nothing like it, and I couldn't stop looking. There was a naked lady on the page, lying on her back with her legs spread open. Her head was far away, you know, like you could barely see it between her spread legs. Johnny grabbed the magazine from me and stared at the same picture for a while. Then he turned the page and we saw another naked lady. This one was bent over. She was staring back at us, this saucy look in her eyes. I'll be damned if we didn't look at every single one of the pictures in that magazine. Afterwards we were really sweaty; like, more sweaty than normal.

Then Johnny said, 'We should bury this.' I'm not sure why he thought that, or why I thought it was a good idea, but we did like he said. We buried it real deep in the ground by the Joshua tree, and we arranged rocks around it so that we could find it again. We probably would have dug it up again in a few days if we hadn't found something else in the field. Something that made us forget about the magazine until the end of summer.

MY SLUT'S LOFTY WITH SOLID PLUMP EGGS

[AFTER E.E CUMMINGS *MY GIRL'S TALL WITH HARD LONG EYES*]

By Hedda Estensen

my slut's lofty with solid plump eggs
as she lays, with her firm banana bundle maintaining
nothing on her leaf, right for being knocked out
is her tough mind and soul smashed with thunder
like a pallid lightning string, when she shows her banana peel
a stiff banana peel at times
bisexually go transparent through me sensational spikes,
and the depressed metal of her grapes block up
my grass through asphalt make a cut – my bitch is massive
and captured, with sticky out branches just like a bush
that's spent all of its cycle on a hill,
and is going to faint. When we forbiddingly hit the ground
with these stems sunset bounds and hooks
for the pseudonym, and to sin on my features and my shell

FLATHEAD

By Emily Parsons

I was six the first time my dad took me flathead fishing on the coast. Just me and him, bobbing by the beach in his rusty tinny.

He woke me before sunrise and helped me into my jeans and jumper. I rubbed sleep from my eyes and looked at the warm covers he'd pulled me from.

I sat back on my bed while he packed the car, fell asleep on the warm pillow and woke up in the front seat of his white Ford ute with the sun flickering through the trees. I sipped chocolate milk, wiped my snotty nose on my sleeves and watched the brown dirt go sandy. Birds slept on power lines.

We wore matching jackets. Bright red. If either of us fell in, we'd see the other in the black water before the sharks got us. His words. They made me shiver. But he ran his big hands through my hair, said he was kidding and laughed until I did too.

Dad tapped along to the ute stereo. He'd fall out of time, get mad at himself and all red in the face. I laughed until he threatened to make me walk home. We were silent for a minute, then I did a milky burp and he stank out the car with one of his sour farts. I danced in my seat and he drummed to the Split Enz cassette tape. The wind flicked my hair.

The air was still cold when we pushed the boat into the harbour. I got water in my boots and Dad threw a blanket over my lap when I shivered.

We sped through the mouth of the river, and were birthed into the expansive sea. I felt small. A red dot in the world of blue around me. I bit my lip, cracked my toes, hugged my knees and felt like crying.

The engine stopped. Someone started singing in a small voice. 'When I was a young boy, I wanted to sail 'round the world, that's the life for me, living on the sea...' I looked at Dad. He smiled and sang the next lines loud and out of tune. His voice echoed on the sand dunes. '...spirit of a sailor, circumnavigates the globe, the lust of a pioneer, will acknowledge no frontier.' I giggled and stopped shivering.

He showed me how to thread a prawn onto a hook in the way that attracts fish best. I watched his hard hands do the delicate work. He helped me throw the line into the water.

I asked him how long 'til we caught a fish. He said it could take hours.

He told me about the last fishing trip he took with his father. How they sat on the water all day, and they were about to turn in when Pop got a bite. A fighter. A big fish that Pop wrestled in the boat and under the waves.

I asked him if Pop had won. He looked at his knuckles, winced, said the fish was too strong, Pop didn't make it out of the water.

Then Dad went quiet.

The sea rocked us in the tinny, like Dad used to rock me to sleep in winter. I felt calm, until I felt sick and sent a cloud of chocolate milk into the water.

I counted the holiday homes along the coastline. They were tall, white, and poked out of the sand dunes like gravestones. We weren't too far from shore, we could swim back if we needed.

A long jetty jutted from the coast to meet us. A man stood at the end. His brown coat flitted in the wind. He held a clay jar that he turned, over and over, tracing the lip with his fingers.

Dad was focused on the sea, so I watched the man. He stood with his chin to his chest. His shoulders shook. He knelt down, took the lid off the jar, kissed the side and tipped it forward. A puff of ash fell and was caught by the wind before it could reach the water. And then came the rest, like a grey column, straight down.

The jar splashed a little and sank to the bottom. The man leaned forward, rested his head on the splintered deck. His hands stretched in front and dangled over the edge, like a man in prayer. He stayed like that for a while.

I heard a whoop behind me. I looked as Dad pulled a long flathead from the water. It wriggled at my feet until he slipped a knife behind its eyes. With a pulse of blood, it was dead. He told me to put the fish in the ice bucket behind me. I pulled it onto my lap, ran my fingers over the orange and brown scales. Cool and slimy.

There was a shout. A splash. I looked to the jetty. The man was in the water, pressing down on it. Trying to stay afloat. He yelled at us that he couldn't swim. He yelled at us to help.

We were frozen.

He did nothing. We watched the man drowning and Dad did nothing. He just sat on the edge of his bench, mouth open, ready to scream or be sick. Face white and those great brown hands turning the fishing rod into splinters. Sounded like bones being crushed.

I watched the man grow tired. I watched him give up. I lost him in the grey water. His brown coat floated as he sank into the waves.

I looked down at my hands. I had pushed my fingers into the belly of the flathead. The blood pooled in my palms, my lap, my boots. My brows twitched. I blinked hard to stop my eyes stinging.

I looked at Dad. He looked at the sinking coat. I wanted him to say something. To do something. Dive into the water and pull the man onto the boat. We weren't that far away. I wasn't afraid of a dead body.

I wanted him to pull the blanket over my shoulders and

tell me it was all OK. Kiss my forehead, scratch my nose with his stubble, sing loud and out of tune.

He was silent. He started the motor and we headed to shore.

I held that bloody fish all the way home.

POLAR BEAR SEQUENCE PART 3

By Harry Godwin

MY LADY OF SHALOTT
By Nanou Blair Gould

My name is Dylan Jones, after my grandfather, Dylan Jones: a bipolar alcoholic. I never met the man but apparently I have his strong will and high cheekbones.

The woman in the hospital bed beside my mother called her sprog Peony Delilah Pea.

'Imagine life with a name like that!' cried Debs. She's my mother. She tells that story a lot. I always wonder whether she meant Peony or me.

I don't doubt my parents love me. My old man graciously took a blow for the family by accepting a job offer as mortgage adviser, tearing us from our little village in Wales to live in a suburb just outside Edinburgh. Debs said I'd benefit from a new and 'cultured' background. As if mankind hasn't sabotaged life enough with conventions without inflicting them on its children. Tell anyone that and you're called 'pretentious'. Unless you're an art student. They thrive on the pretentious, which is why I'm an art student. Which is why I painted 'Earth's Sabotage' for my final portfolio piece.

I brought the first sketches into class that morning, arranging them over three sheets of paper. On the first page a bush of green stems in full, red bloom. On the second I drew the same bush infested with greenfly. On the third the festering petals curled and browned, leaves splattered with fly repellent, rotting at the stem. I imagined each painting on a 100 × 75 cm canvas of rough spun cloth.

Our lecturer Harris Gulliver asked us to pitch our ideas to the class.

Sasha pitched first. She unrolled a blown-up photograph of her boyfriend and herself, reclining naked on a table, arms and legs locked at awkward angles, one boob flopping out.

'It doesn't have a title yet,' Sasha said. 'I see it as a one-piece undefined shape of interlocking limbs creating warmth and light. I thought about using wax, but...'

I remembered sex with Sasha. It was meant as a quick fumble on her carpet, but back then she already fancied her naked body a work of art. She swayed before me, easing off her tights, her dress, her bra, asking how it made me feel. Out of respect I remained silent, and afterwards bolted for the door.

I am a bastard, a sexist. I am frightened of letting go: arrogant, starving myself of the beauty life offers, wallowing in self-pity and pessimism. Or so Sasha says.

She's wrong. I love the simple beauties of life - why else would my work express disgust at humanity?

Harris Gulliver asked to see my sketches again after the workshop.

'I'm bored,' he said.

I lounged back in my chair, trying to look amused.

'You're bored by my work?'

'Yes.'

'OK.'

The drawings lay exposed between us, like Sasha's bare breasts.

'Do you know why?' asked Harris Gulliver.

'No,' I said.

'Because you haven't-'

'I *have* worked on them.'

Harris held up a hand.

'It's deft handwork, Dylan. But they don't suggest anything.'

'Anger?' I offered.

'Stale anger.'

Debs says that as a kid I could stare at a tree trunk for

hours, tracing a finger along the bark or giving it a quick lick when I thought she wasn't watching. I imagined her flapping the hanky she kept tucked up her cardigan sleeve and wiping my tongue. I do remember Debs finding me crouched over the dirty paddling pool feeling snails creep along the skin of my inner arms. And Mrs Ellis, our neighbour, ringing home to ask why their son was hanging by his arms fifteen feet from the ground from her beach tree. Because I liked the feeling it gave my tummy, I told Debs. She carried me sobbing in to Tony, who put down the *Financial Times* and took me to a therapist to check whether I was soft in the head.

Then that one summer, I began painting. I could do it in private, so it troubled them less. I tasted the bark as I stirred browns and reds, and even when I mixed too much blue and the trees became purple and my brushstrokes became frustrated knife strokes, it helped. Painting became addictive and somehow therapeutic. More so than the shrinks and their questions. It was like I'd said all I needed to say but I couldn't stop and all this stuff came out and it scared me a little. Actually it scared me a lot but I was also intrigued to see what else I could heave up. I sent some paintings to an art school in London. Two weeks later, a letter of acceptance lay on Debs's BIENVENUE! doormat.

'You're recycling something you once felt and won't move on,' Harris Gulliver insisted.

'How do you know I'm not frustrated?' I said and he said, 'I can tell you are. But not from work.'

I liked Harris Gulliver. He was the reason I was doing fine arts. On my first day he clapped my shoulder and called me Fandango. Fandango was the shade of purple I used in all my paintings, but he let me find that out in my own time.

The Harris Gulliver opposite me was the epitome of disappointed grownup: sat straight, head down, observing me over his glasses.

'Well,' I said. 'Tony will be thrilled I can continue the

dynasty of mortgage advisors.'

I stood to leave, rolling up 'Earth's Sabotage' with such feeble bravado I scrunched the paper.

'Dylan,' Harris Gulliver said, 'go ahead and feel sorry for yourself. But I promise you, you will fail.'

I wanted to give him the two fingers, to say that that it was his fault: he was the one who had accepted me on the course. But he didn't mean failing art school, and he knew I knew it.

Harris Gulliver somehow favoured Emily's photo of her little brother lying in a dog basket over 'Earth's Sabotage'. During our field trip to the Tate Britain I trailed behind Emily, curious to understand her inspired perception of the world. But I couldn't keep up with her peroxide bob. I lingered at each painting, delighted to find that several mas-terpieces in gold leaf frames bored me.

'I'm such a sucker for pre-Raphaelite art,' Emily said. We stood in a room of pale maidens with mermaid hair. 'It's the flowing gowns and knights in shining armour. I bet you're a bit of a romantic, Dylan. All broody and Dorian Grey.'

'Immoral and corrupt?' I smirked.

'Hedonistic, like.'

'I do like to indulge in life's pleasures, yes.'

Emily smiled. 'I see how Sasha fit – oh, Dylan, look at her!'

And God, she was beautiful.

From her fingers lifting a chain from the water, to the hand resting delicate and limp in her lap. The gentle curve of her belly and breast, her shoulders slumped but chin held high, unabashed by her grief. Her lips! Soft, full lips parted, and her eyes gazing right at me, full of terrible sadness. Her long auburn hair fluttered on the breeze.

I wouldn't let Emily pull me away. I wanted to get closer, to climb into the cold river water and push aside the reeds, take the chain from her hand and carry her from the frame. But I couldn't move any closer without seeing the brush strokes, exposing her as mere layers of pigment and oil. John William Waterhouse, *The Lady of Shalott*, 1888. Then Emily pushed me on to *Ophelia*, a painting of a transvestite in a wig.

That night, instead of lying awake conjuring up Sasha's tits to avoid churning thoughts in the dark, I saw the Lady gliding towards me through the reeds in her boat.

'Don't hide,' she said. 'Who are you?'

I waded towards her, the water up to my waist.

'Dylan,' I said.

'Dylan,' she said, and the way she sang it made me love Debs and my grandfather so, so much. Not Dy-lun: Dylan Dylan Dylan!

Next day I took a forty-minute detour to Bankside on the way back from the supermarket to visit the *Lady*. For the first time in my life I was sneaking around to visit a woman. I hurried to her room and I sat with my Morrisons bags relishing the thrill of her gaze. Nobody ever looked at me like that. I felt uncomfortable and exposed and excited all at the same time.

And again the next day.

I became paranoid someone would notice the young man with high cheekbones besotted with the *Lady of Shalott*. I tucked a sketchpad under my arm. I would spend fifteen minutes standing in front of her, then sit and try to draw, then stand up again because I couldn't get her right. I tried telling myself it was Waterhouse's artistic ability that fascinated me, not the young woman depicted. Then a man would stop to study the *Lady* longer than *Ophelia* or the naked nymphs and I would stop drawing, annoyed and jealous, until he apologise for standing in my way.

One day she left her frame and entered the world. She sat beside me on the bus, her skin smelling musky and fresh and sweet and spicy. She hurried ahead of me through the park, caught between the red autumn leaves and her red autumn hair and she wandered down my road of dull terraced houses, delighted, pointing at a gnome in this garden, the Moroccan print curtains and herbs in that window.

'What do they mean?' she asked.

I pointed to the house with the gnomes and wind chimes. 'That belongs to a couple dominated by a middle aged female, and that-' I indicated the house next door, 'belongs to homosexuals. And there-'

She laughed, her laugh sweeter and lighter than wind chimes.

I woke without rolling over to scream into the pillow. I kicked back the duvet like I used to on Christmas mornings before racing along the landing to my parent's bedroom. I would stand there, squirming in my dinosaur pyjamas until Tony or Debs deemed it a respectable hour. And although Christmas meant a four-hour cramp around the dining room table with the entire Jones family and a succession of disappointing presents, the excitement got me through. With my Lady watching, the week seemed just as hopeful.

My sudden ability to leave the house early confused my housemates. I told them I went running and they raised their eyebrows at my jeans and shoes. The next morning I left the house in a pair of shorts and trainers. Despite my burning, shaking legs, singeing skin and combusting lungs, the morning run had its appeal. My Lady drifted silently beside me, watching colour gradually bleed back into the city. The more I ran, the more my senses heightened, until I was so high I fell spasming and laughing onto a bench. My Lady spread her arms wide, the daggered sleeves of her gown trailing like wings and her body twirling in a stream of red and white.

'Aren't you cold?' I asked.

'No,' she said, breathless. 'No, Dylan, I feel so much, but not the cold. And you?'

When I lie beside real women staring up at their ceiling, they often ask, 'What are you thinking about?' as if such an invasive question deserves a truthful answer. They want me to look at the ceiling and see the galaxy and fill the emptiness in me with them. You, I say, and they adore me all the more for the lie. But my Lady's questions felt good and exciting, somehow.

'Anger?' she asked. 'Do you feel anger?'

I almost laughed. How could I be angry? I could feel the weight of her fingers on my inner arms, the stirring in my belly, and the scent of her amber hair, like resin on the breeze. I could never reach out and grasp her - not really - but I could feel her. Poor Debs and Tony. I had lived most of my life with people who would never know what it felt like to fall in love with your imagination.

'I feel relief,' I said. And the relief was so sweet that my bastard, arrogant, starving lonely soul didn't feel sorry for itself one bit.

I could almost lick a tree again.

On the morning of our next pitching I drew a private piece, of the glass veranda back in Edinburgh, with all Debs's pottery ducks I hated so much and Tony's M&S suit draped over the ironing board. I drew my Lady of Shalott sat on the sofa, completely out of place in the mundanity. I tweaked her lips ever so slightly so she smiled.

Harris Gulliver asked us to sum up our work in a word.

'Disappointment,' I muttered, holding up 'Earth's Sabotage'.

'Lust,' said Sasha.

'Loss,' said Emily, and suddenly the shot of the boy in the basket made sense.

'Your dog died?' I asked her afterwards.

'We had him put down a few weeks ago.'

I looked at the little boy in crumpled pyjamas.

'I wanted to cry as I took the photo,' Emily said. 'I almost didn't take it.'

'Why did you?'

'We can't be put off by strong feelings if we want to produce honest art.'

'What if we make the feeling up?'

Emily raised an eyebrow. 'All emotions are real, Dylan, even if the subject of them is just an idea. I've never died but I'm still scared of dying. Have you finished 'Earth's Sabotage'?'

'No.' I turned my back on the rest of the class, leaving just enough space for Harris Gulliver's prying eyes, and slid the drawing of my veranda from my file.

'I don't...' Emily frowned, then laughed. 'Dylan, is she – I mean, is that Waterhouse's *Lady*-?'

'No,' I said. 'She's mine. My Lady of Shalott.'

HARK THE HERALD ANGEL

By Steph Vickers

It was the Winter term of '97, my first year of primary school. We made paper snowflakes to hang from the ceiling of Mrs Something-or-Other's classroom, our duffle coats and puffer jackets hung in a line on the wall. Mrs Something-or-Other said words like 'cross', and made us walk down corridors holding hands in pairs. Only a week remained until we broke up for Christmas, and we spent it traipsing to and from the assembly hall, rehearsing for a Nativity play.

It was always the Nativity. We confused it with Noah's Ark and wanted to be giraffes and deer and elephants marching two by two to see the baby Jesus, but Mrs Something-or-Other didn't like to be that unconventional. She already had to cast the same cookie-cutter roles in the same tea-towel costumes every year: A Mary and a Joseph, three wise men, three shepherds, three inn keepers – not one – a few stars and sixteen angels, because Mrs Something-or-Other had a big class that year. She picked me to be an angel.

Everybody got one line. Those lines became the pride of 30 five-year olds, and the plight of my existence. I spoke in Makaton sign language and was mostly mute. Every sentence ended up a battle with my st-st-st-stammer, and after a year of being mockingly called St-st-st-steph, I gave up my voice. A speech therapist visited me every Tuesday morning. Sp-sp-sp-speech therapy because I c-c-c-couldn't speak.

A star will guide you to Bethlehem. That was my line. A st-st-st-star will gu-gu-guide you to-to-Beth-beth-bethlehem. I still wanted to do Noah's Ark; the giraffes wouldn't have to talk.

On Tuesday mornings there were umpteen different ways to say my one little line.

'Perhaps you could put it to a tune?' the speech therapist suggested.

'Sing it?' offered Mrs Something-or-Other. 'Use fillers?'

'Don't count down the other angels,' the speech therapist said. 'Mouth their lines too.'

They could have starred me as the baby Jesus; then all I'd have to do was cry.

When Tuesday afternoons rolled around, I just managed to count every line of every angel. I waited for 'look to the sky for a sign,' as my cue to make a quick escape to the toilet, and the clamour of 30 five-year olds who didn't know the words to We Three Kings to safely slip back in.

The eager parents of the budding stars put the outfits together. Red robes for Mary and Joseph, three Burger King crowns, three striped dressing gowns, and three oversized shirts, a few sprayed-gold cardboard headbands, and sixteen tinsel halos. Thursday's dress rehearsal had the angels balancing on a bench behind the shepherds.

'Speak slowly,' Mrs Something-or-Other soothed.

A s-t-a-r w-i-l-l g-u-i-d-e y-o-u t-o B-e-t-h-l-e-h-e-m.

My dress clung too tight and my halo itched. I said it so slowly that the kid playing Gabriel, anxious to take centre stage, ended up saying it for me.

On Friday morning, thirty sets of parents sat waiting in an assembly hall decked in tinsel and paper snowflakes. Mary, Joseph, all the shepherds, all the kings and all the wise men, the inn keepers, a few stars and fifteen angels walked two-by-two down the corridor and found their places on the stage. I stayed at home with my st-st-st-stammer.

Gabriel got an extra line, and one of the shepherds wore my halo.

THE PLAGUE POPPET

By Emma Riddell

She knock-knocks and soft-pads inside. Glows pale and cold-cheeked in the dim room.

'I am glad to see The Lord keeps you safe, Mary,' she says.

She sets her gloves on the table.

I grunt; her Lord sleeps. It's me keeps us plague-safe; my potions, my knowing. Yet it's not enough, the sickness grows stronger. I bend to my work. Finger bones crackle with each in and out of the needle.

'I have come to see the stitched horror that the women whisper of,' she says. She stinks of church insides: wax, God breath.

I raise up and shake the boar corpse. 'It will gore the pestilence through its heart,' I say. Tusks swing at her, pointed as daggers. She flutters backwards, then steadies and throws out roots. I nod at the other empty skins spread on the ground. 'Hare's ears will hear it coming, a fox's tail brings cunning.'

'We should pray together. I can see this is harmless foolishness, but there are others at the church who call it sinister,' she says.

I tap my foot. 'Your churchman died. People's kneeling brought him no salvation.' I am pleased to use the word. It is her word and it knocks her back.

'Father Thomas already had the pestilence upon him; the tokens wept raw under his armpits,' she says.

I snip the hare's ears and sew them to the boar's head. My hearth fire is as hot as hell. Salt-water slips down her face. The blaze embraces us, murmuring songs of family and feasts long turned cold. The twigs I gather burn poorly, but I use my knowing. All the while babes die and mothers fear, they bring me gifts from their woodpiles. Sides of pig. Bread. But for how long?

'How old are you now, Mary? It seems to me that you were old even when I was a girl,' she says.

'One king restored, one butchered. A pretender, a devil-fucked Scotch, a queen wiser than the each of them,' I say. She pales at the fuck-word. My cat, Malkin, escapes my skirts, grabs the foxtail.

'You live here alone.' She speaks only of men. 'If you came to the church we would feed you. We would see you did not starve.'

'Pah!' I spit on the stones. If she would go I could sew on. She didn't bring kindling, or eggs, or beer. Malkin thinks her here too long. He squats on the table and hisses. She fixes him with her eyes. There is spine in her. Good girl.

'Come to the church, Mary. Pray with me,' she says. Old tales.

I stuff the creature through its belly slit with lavender, thyme and dried oak leaves. It plumps. It stands on the table. Malkin's ears flatten, his eyes are moons. He backs out. Flees into the woods to hunt and crouch out his seed.

I sew on.

I see her gloves are gone. Since when? A cat's blink? Days? Time flows unsteady now: pooling then sluicing away. Malkin sits on my lap, but my hands are too stiff to stroke him. The poppet is done. It lies on the table; a cobbled bag of skins, nothing more.

Old fool.

Then the stitched creature snuffles and rises. It jabs at me; full of hate. The stink! But I will suckle it at the tit if it will drive off the plague.

LACHRYMOSE
By Haley Jenkins

Wireless idea thrumming lackadaisical for our canon,
Womb haemorrhaging neophytes tearing the surface
    archive shelf.

Neurotic trend supplies brilliance that breaks
As scribbles advertise luck and suffering over commas.

Nod to the sonnet, where we will procrastinate
Whittle semantic hazards that navigate intellectual gusto.

Novelise those tomb sentiments, investigate binary dactyls,
Semiprecious Flarfers offshoot socialism, literary skeletons
    are nebulous.

Nonsense turning the tide around Brain's genocide,
Awaken writers' harlequin fidelity, hibernating telepathic
    doppelgangers.

Neonatal thoughts that wept here mirroring cadence
Ebullient themes struggle here earning brevity.

After poetry loves that infertility, functioning over chaos,
Womb haemorrhaging neophytes tearing the surface
    archive shelf.

THE END OF A PIER

By Nicholas Elliot

I stand alone on the beach, under the indulgent moon, holding the plastic figurine. The cigarette butts at my feet sink into the wet sand. The tide claws at my toes. I shout into the darkness and the waves hiss. I step back and use my big toe to write in the sand; it will be washed away by the tide before anyone can read it.

I write that I am alive and dead.

That morning was our annual trip to the beach. Every September for ten years, me and my wife packed up the same windbreak, the same towels, the same brand of Factor 30 sunscreen. Charlotte wore the same maroon all-in-one bathing suit that stretched halfway down her thighs. Her figure was something to hide and she knew it.

The annual beach trip was always the same week as our anniversary. This year I got her a new vacuum cleaner. The old one was only a year or so old but she had exhausted it. The whirring and humming of the vacuum accounted for most of the noise in our house.

She got me plain black socks.

At the beach we lay two yards apart, my head closer to the sea, hers to the car park. She applied layer after layer of sunscreen to her pale skin. I laid on my front and waited for the sun to fidget through the clouds and redden my shoulders and neck. Children made sandcastles and ran away from chasing waves. The louder their laughter got, the louder Charlotte slapped and lathered the lotion on her skin. It was the tenth year we had visited the beach as a married couple and the ninth year since I had been pronounced sterile.

Useless.

Under the moon, I write in the sand that I am the nanosecond before infinity. I am pi's last digit. I am Schrodinger's cat.

When I awoke on the beach, the sun was going down. Charlotte was asleep and Frisbees flew with seagulls in the salted air. That's when I saw her. She sat at the end of the pier with her feet dangling just above the sea's reach. Frustrated waves broke underneath her. Her head was bowed so her midnight purple hair hung over her face. I had taken three steps toward her before I realised what I was doing. I wanted to lie back down. I wanted to return to the towel slightly distant from Charlotte's and sleep in the safety, in the normalness. The girl on the pier was like big moons on the tide.

I write in the sand that I am two identical snowflakes. I am the back of the *Mona Lisa*'s head.

I stood behind the girl as the waves grasped her feet and rejoiced under the pier. Her back was smooth and milky white. I thought of the cluster of moles that bisected Charlotte's shoulder blades and I wanted to touch the girl's skin. My hand hesitated an inch above her back when she spoke.

'Hello.'

I withdrew my hand.

'Hello,' I replied.

The girl kept her head bowed and facing the sea.

'I love the sea. Do you?' she said. My mouth opened but no words. 'The smell, the sound, the endlessness. It's therapeutic, but also exciting. Sit down. If you like.' She patted the spot next to her.

I lowered myself and mirrored her pose, my head bowed and feet submerged. She slid one side of her hair behind her ear and I saw her face. She had shallow dimples and arched candle wax lips. Her smile silenced the giggling children, the seagull battle plan, the breaking waves.

'My name is Alice. What's yours?'

'Erwin,' I said, sucking in my gut and straightening my back to broaden my chest.

'You're kind of cute, aren't you Erwin?'

I touched my chin to one shoulder then the other and hoped my red face would pass for sunburn.

'This is one of my favourite places to come. The sea is a good partner. Are you a good partner, Erwin?'

I thought I heard Charlotte's squeaky throat clear behind me but it was just a seagull.

'I might be. Who knows?' I said.

We sat there until the sea had risen halfway up my shins. Now and then I checked to see if Charlotte had woken up. She had rolled from her back to her front, maybe in her sleep, maybe not. The sun was low and the abandoned ruins of sandcastles cast long shadows over the beach.

'Meet me here tonight at ten,' I said.

'Here?'

'Yeah, here at the end of the pier. We can listen to the sea. And maybe we'll find out if I'm a good partner.'

Alice raised her feet from the water then drowned them again.

'Okay. Here, at ten. It's a date.'

I write in the sand that I am the sexual tension between captive pandas. I am a melting ice cap. I am my dead ejaculate.

When Charlotte and I got home I put the windbreak and towels away then went to the back garden for a smoke. Smoking inside was prohibited. I sat downstairs and looked at the corner of carpet behind the television. The vacuum cleaner roamed upstairs and I passed it and sat on the bed as Charlotte cleaned downstairs. Then I sat in front of the grandfather clock in the hall and willed time along. Charlotte rammed the vacuum cleaner into the side of my feet to get to the particles of dirt underneath. I stood up and walked over to where Charlotte's precious child was plugged into the wall. I pulled the cord out and threw it to the ground.

Charlotte turned and waited for an explanation.

'You really are a soulless bitch aren't you?' I said. She gripped the vacuum cleaner handle. 'It's been nine years since we had sex. Ten since I've been happy. You know what? I've had enough.'

I walked past her, pulled on my jacket and opened the front door. I glared at the corner of carpet behind the television.

'She's too pretty for you,' Charlotte called from the hall. 'That girl on the pier. Yes I saw you, and no I don't care.'

I sat in the car for a moment and thought she might come after me, apologise and lead me to the bedroom for the first time in years. I stared at the front door and waited until I heard the hum of the vacuum cleaner.

I write in the sand that I exist in a vacuum. I fall at the same rate as feather and brick. I am the rule that proves the exception.

The sea wipes the words away.

I walked along the dark sand, smoking a cigarette. In the distance the faint outline of the pier rested under moonlight. Nine fifty-five. Alice wasn't there yet. She wasn't sat with her bare feet soaking in the sea. She wasn't checking her reflection in its wet mirror. I inched along the length of the pier and imagined her moaning when I laid her down and the cold damp wood of the pier touched her milky white back.

When I reached the end of the pier my mouth fell open and the cigarette dropped out, bounced off the wood and dissolved into the wet blackness. I looked down: read it over and over again. Fragments of shell laid out for me. The shell letters spelt a single word. *Sorry.*

I sat in the car outside the house. I could hear one of Charlotte's audio books, roaring. My departure had not disrupted her routine. The living room window was left at a crack to air my smell out of the house. I slipped out of the car, leaving the door ajar. I knew the stiff front door lock would creak, even above the audio book, so I worked the living room window open, got my knee up and placed my foot on the windowsill. The air in the living room was thick and hot with Summer Breeze and other cleaning smells. I crept over to the corner behind the television and lifted up the carpet. I shuffled the loose floorboard to one side and plunged my hand into the gap. I pulled them up and put them in my jacket.

I left through the window and got back into the car. As I drove back to the beach they muttered in my pocket.

That is where I am now, writing in the sand with my big toe. I write that I am redundant.

I turn the plastic figurine over in my hand. The bottoms of their shoes are still worn from standing on our wedding cake. Their plastic smiles have not faded.

I throw the smiling couple into the sea and step forwards, so the sea can grasp my ankles.

SECTIONED

By Heidi Larsen

1 The pub was filled with people wearing a hundred percent wool, and faded leather boots with tired shoelaces.

2 They wore eighteen carat gold earrings and glasses that were either round and covered only their eyeballs or had thick, black frames and reached from eye brow to cheekbone.

3 A woman sat down at the bar. She had no facial expression and no make-up.

4 She wore a camel coloured dress that reached her toes; the texture of her nipples showed through the polyester. 'Light your dress.'

5 'What can I get you?' the bartender said.

6 The woman stared at a foursome sitting opposite the bar. The two men gesticulated and showed their teeth as they talked.

7 The women sitting with them were slender, with boyish figures and pretty faces.

8 They wore red lipstick and had shiny hair, half of it tied in a knot on top of their heads.

9 One of them laughed. The other joined in, stroked the guy next to her's arm and said 'Oh Alan, you're hilarious.'

I had coffee with my brother, Carl, and I told him I didn't like the way the barista was looking at me.
'Maybe he fancies you,' Carl said.
I said I was sure he had an agenda, and anyway, Frank Ocean was the man for me. Carl laughed.
He said 'Honey, I think I saw Frank in the men's room, he was peeing in a urinal and he had a doughnut around his dick.'
I said 'Don't be silly, Frank didn't go to the men's room.'
Carl said 'I'm pretty sure he did...'
So Frank and I got up and left. We have avoided Carl since then!

10 The conversation in the pub shifted from politics and economy to art and poetry.

11 The foursome became two couples; one held hands under the table, the other guy rested his hand on the inside of his woman's thigh.

12 The music changed from indie to ballads.

13 'Can I get you anything?' the bartender asked again.

14 The woman continued to stare.

15 'Is he late?' a man at the bar slurred. 'Is your date late?' He pronounced the words slowly and clearly.

16 He lifted his glass to his mouth and beer ran down his chin.

17 The woman turned around. 'They said to meet him here,' she said. 'My boyfriend is Frank Ocean. This is where I needed to go.'

18 Ears turned to the conversation.

19 'Frank Ocean, the famous singer?' someone said.

20 'They may have lied,' the woman said. 'I'm becoming sceptical of these shoes.'

2 It was better than marriage; it meant more than a certificate or a blessing from the devil.

2 'Only a bad religion can make me feel the way I do,' Frank said.

3 The ceremony was simple; I took off my ballet pumps and he took off his sandals – a sign of volunteering.

4 I burned his shoes and he burned mine to make it irreversible.

5 'We can walk where we want now. They can't tell us where to go. My shoes, always telling me to run away from you, I'm glad they burnt in hell!' Frank said.

6 He kissed me and my bone

I dreamt that they had already strangled me with their shoelaces; the priests, the mullahs and the monks. I see the intention in their eyes when they throw shoes; they aim at my temples. I run away when I see a religious person, I avoid the situation, but in my dream they finally did it. They killed me. It was the floor that gave me the dream. It said 'Be sceptical of beds, they may be in on it.' So I slept on the floor and I understood; I had to go to the mountains where no shoes could get to me.

marrow vibrated.

7 Taking your shoes off together to gain trust and clarity is the most honest and loving thing two people can do.

8 The trees smelled of hamster crap and shone yellow over us.

9 We sat in the glimmer and took off our clothes.

10 Frank told me he would never put them back on and he would never leave me.

11 For the first time, my heart wasn't weighing my body down.

12 We made love under the trees.

13 I squeezed and released 'til I had pumped Frank's soul out, blended it with mine and vacuum-packed them around us.

14 My ribcage bumped into my lungs and made my heart shake, sending shivers through my body and curling my toes.

15 I was never happier.

3 The ladies' room smelled of cloistered knickers and sweat.

2 Christine heard whispering from a cubicle and smiled at the thought of two women finding each other.

3 'I can't tell you the truth about my disguise, I can't trust no one,' Frank said.

4 Although their relationship was fresh, Christine could no longer remember what it was like to be a single person, waking up alone in an empty flat, not having to shower on weekends, going a whole day without talking to someone and not having to shave for months because no one noticed until hair stuck out through her t-shirt.

5 Carl said he thought it sad that people in relationships started identifying themselves as one of a pair.

'Set fire to your shoes and walk with the devil because you are a sinner.'

6 Christine didn't mind being one of a pair as long as she always had someone to hug.

7 She put lipstick on and rubbed her lips together.

8 The whispering got louder and spread to the other stalls.

9 The music from the pub disappeared and the whis-

pering became yellow air. 'If they find you, you will be prosecuted.'

10 Christine heard stiletto clicks, the bathroom door closing and a key being turned.

Bad Christine Bad Christine
Bad Christine Bad Christine
Bad Christine Bad Christine
Bad Christine Bad Christine
Bad Christine Bad Christine
Bad Christine Bad Christine

11 In the mirror she saw that a yellow skinned woman in a yellow suit had walked in.

12 She turned her attention to her makeup bag.

13 The cubicle doors opened, and six women came out.

14 They wore yellow suits and dresses, had hair in different shades of orange and skin in different yellows.

15 Their eyeballs were parsnip, their fingernails fish oil, and their teeth Pelagic Sea Snake.

16 They walked touse of the word "constitution", as mission statements could conceivably be modifiedwards Christine forming a half circle around her.

17 'Hello?' Christine felt her shoulders shrink and her heart beat faster.

18 No one answered.

19 A puff of air brushing her neck felt like a hand, her skin tightened and her breathing hardened.

20 Christine put her hand to her neck, looking for buttons to unfasten but there were none.

21 Christine looked for an escape but there was none.

22 One of the women pulled out a knife case.

23 Christine looked for a weapon but there was none.

24 Christine searched for protection and found a towel.

25 She wrapped it around her hand, planning to use it as a shield should someone try to stab her.

26 The yellow women reached her before she could secure it.

27 The towel fell to the floor and four of the women grabbed a limb each and forced her to the ground.

28 The other three took off her shoes and tights.

29 They ripped up her new dress like it was crepe paper.

30 Christine lost feeling in

her limbs but still felt clammy fingers leaving prints of sweat as the wo-men removed her under-wear.

31 She screamed and cried but no sound left her mouth. 32 The knife case was opened and one of the women pulled out a paint-brush.

33 One of the women went into a cubicle and came back with a bucket of yellow paint.

34 Christine tensed each of her muscles, felt her head simmer and her stomach muscles sting but she could not move.

35 Christine felt blood drizzle down her throat from her vocal cords but she could not scream.

36 Christine felt the inside of her thighs get warm and then cold.

37 The woman dipped the paintbrush between her legs and mixed it with paint.

38 Christine realised she had wet herself.

39 The women painted un-der her feet, between her toes, all the way up to her hairline.

40 Then they turned her over and started at her feet again, painting between her buttocks and poking the brush into her ears, 'til every pore was covered.

41 With each brushstroke Christine's chest tightened more as her skin cells were smothered.

42 The redness in her face shone through just enough to create orange cheeks, so the women gave her another coat. 43 Then they left.

44 If minutes or hours went by before she got up, Christine didn't notice.

45 Tears rolled down her cheeks and, to her relief, paint ran with them.

46 She filled shaking hands with water and splashed her yellow body. She sat in the sink and poured handful after handful of water over herself until she was paint-free.

47 She dried herself with toilet paper and sheltered under the hand dryer.

4 Christine and Frank sat at the crowded bar. 2 Frank wore a blue hoodie and sunglasses.

3 'Your boyfriend is so cosy looking,' a tipsy lady said.

4 She smiled, showing all her teeth but no facial lines.

5 People laughed and one girl said, 'Aww, I wish I had a life-sized Smurf to cuddle.'

6 A blue man took a sip of his beer and said 'My blue trainers smell, you want them in your face? You wanna smell my shoes?'

Bad religion Bad religion
Bad religion Bad religion
Bad religion Bad religion
Bad religion Bad religion
Bad religion Bad religion
Bad religion Bad religion

7 People laughed nervously, some rolled their eyes.

8 Christine grabbed Frank's hand and noticed how clammy it was.

9 She stroked his arms and discretely rubbed off the sweat.

10 'I told you they want to split us up,' Christine said. 'Can't you see that?'

11 Her heart beat faster.

12 Frank looked at Christine. 'I won't let them.'

13 A short man with long hair offered a distraction by standing up and reading a self written poem about pretentiousness.

14 He laughed as he read it but he was the only one.

15 Christine nudged Frank. 'Please can we go? I don't feel good about this.'

16 'Is there a more pretentious word for pretentious?' the man said when he had finished his poem.

17 The two women next to him laughed.

18 The short man stood up again. 'I have a deeper poem, about my parents' divorce.'

19 He paused and lowered his eyebrows. 'I must warn you, it's rather dark.'

20 He sat down again and stared into his whisky glass.

21 The women who had laughed stood up and hugged him, breasts meeting face. 'Let he who is without sin throw the first stone. Let she who is the sinner be prosecuted.'

22 He put his arms around them.

23 Another man stood up and slammed his glass down, making the liquid jump out, unnoticed, onto someone's sleeve.

24 'I, I have written a poem

about my uncle's suicide.'
His voice shook.
25 A girl squeezed his arm.
26 He took a deep breath
and continued. 'I just wish…
I could hold him in my arms
once more. It should have
been me!'
27 Christine nudged Frank
again. 'Please, Frank. This
doesn't feel right.'
28 'Christine, please,' Frank
said. 'I'm enjoying the poetry.'
29 A woman in a turquoise
knitted jumper covered her
mouth and whispered, 'He
used to hold his uncle in his
arms?' Her friends giggled.
30 Something hit Christine's
shin.
31 She looked down and saw
a trainer on the floor.
32 'This one's for you, as-
shole!' the blue man said
and threw his other shoe.
33 'Poet fight!' someone
shouted.
34 'Yes!' the crowd chanted.
'Poet fight, poet fight.'
35 The shoeless man was
joined by four priests in blue
capes.
36 'Oh shit, Frank. This is it.'
Christine said.
37 She hid her face in

Frank's hoodie. It smelled of
fart and she could hear his
heart pounding.
38 Silence.
39 The priests started unty-
ing their laces.

5 The purple light from
the trees created an il-
lusion of warmth in the
December night, but
Christine was cold and the
stain remover froze on her
naked body.
2 'It didn't work, Frank. I
still need to be prosecuted
for my sins.'
3 'Shh, we gotta share body
heat,' he said.
4 Christine held Frank's
blue hands, cold like the
blade of an axe.
5 She gathered warm air
from her lungs and blew on
them like she was fogging a
mirror. Only cold air came
out.
6 She placed his hands under her breasts; his blue skin
mixed with her pink skin,
causing purple to spread
across her stomach.
7 She pulled her arms to her
chest and her shoulders to
her ears. The tension
reached her head and she

could hear her heart beating inside her skull.

8 'Christine, I'm cold.'

9 Christine gripped Frank's arms and raised them in the

A woman walked in to the gas station the other day. She had no shoes on. I asked her if I could help her with anything. She said, 'Yes, you can free me from my sin, and get me straightened out.'

I laughed. She said, 'The cow needs to be released from its milk because you are not cancer, you have cancer and sometimes I feel like I can't run anymore.' She looked at me with raised eyebrows and wide pupils and screamed. People turned around and stared at me like I had hurt her or something. I started to sweat; I didn't know what to say. My manager came over and asked her if she was OK.

She said. 'No, I'm not OK. I'm so scared I can tell you the till is bleeding.'

I frowned. 'What the fuck?'

She took a step back and my manager waved me away. He talked to her in a calm voice and said, "Do you want to tell me about that?"

'Alright, alright,' the crazy lady said. 'When it cramps its muscles contracts and creates friction so that the iron can straighten the shirt without burning.'

There was silence, and the woman ran out. We had to call the police.

---

air. They were shaking but he held them up while she pulled off his jumper.

10 She removed his t-shirt and hugged him.

11 He shivered.

12 Heat grew between them while the wind nagged around their bodies.

13 Frank slipped one hand up Christine's back and untied the knot in her hair.

14 A long, thick blanket enveloped them.

15 Christine opened Frank's belt buckle and slipped her hand down his pants.

16 Cold, shrunk. She looked at him.

17 'I can't feel my toes, Frank,' she said.

18 'Here, babe,' Frank took off his jeans and laid them on the ground. 'Sit down and put your feet on my stomach.'

19 He rubbed Christine's feet and wrapped his jumper around her.

20 He kissed her with cold lips.

21 He knocked his forehead against hers. A shoe hit him in the head.

22 'Fuck!' he said.

23 They looked around and saw a group of blue monks gliding towards them.

24 They had a trolley full of shoes.

25 The monks threw trainers, boots and stilettos.

26 As they got closer, they threw with greater confidence, aiming for heads.

27 Frank took Christine's hand and led her to a side gate.

'You must be prosecuted and electrocuted for all the sins you have committed. Light yourself.'

28 They were too cold to run, so Frank opened the lid to a public plastic waste container and helped Christine in.

29 They curled together like Siamese foetuses, guarding each other's temples.

30 Christine rubbed Frank's arms and kissed his nose, chin and Adam's apple.

30 She shook in rhythm with his heartbeat and her nose stung from holding back tears.

31 'We need to hide in the mountains,' she said. 'But if they get us now, at least we'll die together and we won't have to do this anymore.

6 Frank drummed on the bar with his forefingers.

2 He kissed Christine on the head and smiled and nodded to people who smiled back.

3 'Only a bad religion can have me feeling the way I do.' Frank said.

4 'Frank, I don't like the way these people stare at me. Why did you bring me here?' Christine said.

5 Her heart tightened, once, then skipped a contraction, making it feel like it drooped to her lungs.

6 Frank opened a carrier bag full of doughnuts.

7 He lined them up across the bar and said, 'Dig in, good folks.'

8 Hungry men congregated at the bar.

9 Christine watched their backs curl over the doughnuts and their heads bob back and forth as they ate.

10 Conversation was replaced with the sound of smacking lips.

11 Christine slid her hands over Frank's back muscles, applying pressure with her palms from his lower back up to his shoulders, and started rubbing his neck.

12 She leaned in to smell

him.

13 His jumper smelled like it was still attached to the sheep; the hamster smell soothed the smell of iron.

14 Frank elbowed Christine in the ribs and continued chewing.

15 Christine squatted and pressed her hands against her ribcage to ease the stinging, which had spread to her lungs and abdominal muscles, to her throat, to her jaw muscles and down to her chest.

16 She gagged.

17 Christine held her breath for as long as she could, then took shallow breaths, keeping her ribcage from elevating and the stinging from getting a grip around her heart.

18 She felt blood thicken in her veins.

19 She stayed on the floor 'til a woman whose boyfriend was eating doughnuts helped her up.

20 She smiled and said, 'What can you do, eh?'

21 'Frank...' Christine said with her lungs' remaining oxygen.

22 Frank didn't seem to hear.

23 The woman shrugged and walked away.

24 Christine's arms and legs were swollen; her heart had pumped the blood from her stomach and bungee jumped inside her.

25 She grabbed hold of a chair and stomped on the floor to feel the texture of the cold stone tiles under her feet.

26 The blood rushed to her head and she started to sweat.

27 Christine looked around the pub.

28 People were concentrating on eating doughnuts or conversing about the weather.

29 Except for the Pope.

30 The Pope was sitting at a table next to the toilets, drinking beer straight from the jug.

31 He stared at her and took off his shoes.

32 'Frank!' Christine yelled.

33 Frank looked up from his doughnut.

34 He frowned at Christine.

35 He loosened his shoelaces.

WHISTLING THROUGH TEETH
& EATING CHOCOLATE ORANGE
By Rebecca Rosier

-

In the light kicked in
next to the passing train windows
next to the cows

That long gravel path
made short by a
red 2-inch book and a restless lust.
together with
the inevitable passing of time
-

I was full of me
& you seemed so too.
Favourite white
every crease new explorable.
The wheelbarrow on your porch
still harbours pale rhubarb.
-

In the room of your new house
carpet upon carpet
smelling of a massage room
impressions of a well trodden pile
what an empty house seemed.
Fixed my hair
fixed my eyeliner
cleaned my hands.

What was then
was then,
but it felt like now.
Only now-
-

In my bed I wore a roll-neck
two soft yellow bed socks.
Scratched through white blinds.
-

The more he clicks his knuckles
the closer I get to the blue
-

footsteps, doors
corridors, walls,
numbers, names,
restaurants, walls.
Each the last.
-

I took my time with a million parcels,
over a million situations,
over one half of a polo.
A perfect crescent. Powdery and
sweet.
-

I spent my hours
waiting for buses
to get somewhere
Then waiting for buses
to get out for there.
I marked my days
Handfuls of sugar puffs.
Cups of pale camomile
rubbing my nose on shirt cuffs
made washing worthwhile
-

Hired and blue.

Belonging to nobody and
somebody un-particular.
We took our voices
& there was singing.
-

The pink-shoed lady pulled up the blinds
as the District Line pulled in
like then.
Unwrapping plates with a satisfying tear
finding a position on a velvet chair
holding the door with a bright red wedge
finding myself in an empty bed

With nothing but rhymes in my empty head.
-

You hate my breadknife
it's all I own
but then you'd hate any knife
I'd chosen alone
-

Against the brown coarse
a silver siren
it's not mine.
Reflecting the space between A, E
"Just…"
if only, but not yet, not for me.
-

My hair was knotted today-
big and round and coarse.
MY EYES WERE JEWELS.
I wore a tutu.
It was   -nice. But
you said
I looked pregnant in it.
Thanks.
As it is as it is:

you'd hate my midwife
you'd say so too.
you'd hate any midwife
chosen without you.

IN A DIFFERENT LIGHT

By Sean Wai Keung

1)
I looked up at
you from my chair felt a wave
of inspiration
from *Midsomer Murders*
I began to think

about blood & knives &
thick southern English accents
'accidents' involving aristo-
cratic fortunes and rev-
erends and poisoned marmalade in jars

behind you a shadow
grew thicker & bolder
than the 28watt bulb
dripping & spluttering &
gasping

my eyes glazed
over because
you gave me that
look that says & said

"put the bloody kettle on already for fucks sake, peter"

how is it I
married you fifteen

years ago yet never noticed
that scar line around your neck?

2)
On a rainy day
with our window
open to let light in
a bit outside
a strangers cat cree-
ley seeking shelter &
warmth & leftover
things could have been so different

WE MET IN OUTER SOUNDSPACE
By Audrey Jean

and then i thought about
the way his voice
      asking the terrible nothing with
      a tenderness only deeply soaked beings
            into themselves and the
            dust asterisms
      can complete
was able to echo my own—

he must also have been
stargazing while keeping his eyes
closed
      laced with particles of
      human abstraction and
            disturbingly sentient dark matter,
      dream-sharing into oblivion—
always dying

FIXED IN AMBER

By Madeleine Morris

Malaga, June 21, 1990

The marine bows stiffly and releases his armful of red carnations onto the cafe's stainless steel table. They blanket it, cascading onto the pavement beneath.

'Flores bonitas para una chica bonita.' He speaks broken Spanish with a Southern drawl.

'It's okay, I speak English,' I say.

'Pretty flowers for a pretty girl.' He's young and his smile is bright white and uncertain.

Malaga, June 21, 1937

Tethered to each other by a single rope, the blindfolded prisoners are pulled through the empty streets in the dappled light of dawn. For the most part, the denizens of this war-torn city are still in their beds, sweating through sheets of nervous dreams.

The flowers aren't specifically for me. On his very first shore leave off the USS *Theodore Roosevelt*, he has wandered up from the port, through the flower market. He's taken the advice offered by his fellow marines, veterans of the Med Cruise: 'Wanna get laid? Buy a shitload of flowers at the market, bro. Then dump them at the feet of the first chick you meet.'

Either I'm the first attractive one he's stumbled upon, or he's a good judge of women and decided I'm the most receptive. In either case, he's perfect for my purposes. He doesn't know that I've been expecting him, or someone just like him. I keep him waiting minutes without a response; it's what he expects. He's exactly what I need: a soldier. Young but with no blood on his hands yet. I give the chair opposite a nudge with my foot. 'Would you like to sit down?'

There are few witnesses to the blind chain's passing. And fewer still who allow themselves to be seen to witness it. But there is at least one who lives to tell what happened. The captain who leads them has fortified himself with a little aguardiente. The burning cigarette clamped between his lips bounces with his steps. Until he stops, pulls it from his fleshy mouth, and kills it on the cobblestones.

'This will do,' he says to the three soldiers with rifles bringing up the rear. 'Line them up.'

We sit and talk at the cafe. Jim the marine drinks beer to shore up his courage and I drink Coke, silently reviewing the details of my plan. As the afternoon wears on, he invites me to a movie. They're showing a rerun of *Apocalypse Now* with subtitles at the Cine Victoria. Above the sound of explosions and the snaps of people cracking sunflower seeds between their teeth, he strokes my bare thigh and offers a running commentary on the authenticity of the film's armaments.

When he gets up the nerve to kiss me, I let him. He tastes of hops. With courtly persistence, callused fingers thread between the buttons of my blouse. Fingertips slip into the cup of my bra and coax a nipple that needs no coaxing.

I want his youth and his strength, his freshly forged adult body, his optimism and his desire. Aren't they all young and raw? I look up at the screen and remember all the history I've ever read, ever heard from people old enough to remember. My father said if you read too much history, you get caught there, in the past. But he's wrong; we're all caught in history, whether we read it or not. We keep doing the same awful things, over and over again. But I can stop it. I've been working it all out and I know if I do everything just right, I can make the murderous wheel grind to a halt.

We leave the cinema, blush-cheeked and breathless. The sun has not yet set. I need darkness for the magic I plan to perform, and so I take him to a quaint little bodega on a side street off Calle Larios. I feed him fresh sardines in brine and roasted red peppers, filling his glass with Rioja until his laugh has lost its jagged edge and his smile gentles.

He's a sweet boy caught up in a terrible machine. For him, history is just something he had to endure in high school. He doesn't know he's trapped in amber, like the rest of us.

In this quiet little alley, no one speaks, although Arturo, the youngest of the prisoners, is weeping softly. But no one begs for a mercy they know they will not get. No one collapses, or pleads, or tries to break away. Ramon, Carlos, the two Juans – the elder and the younger – Antonio, and Paco all knew this would be their end the moment they were captured. This is how it always ends for the losers – up against the wall of a slumbering house in some unfamiliar barrio.

Mellow-eyed, he turns sombre. 'You sure are beautiful.' He traces his thumb over my cheek. 'Not the kind of girl who gives it up on a first date, I'm guessing.'

I hadn't expected chivalry. This is awkward. I smile at him and arch an eyebrow. 'You don't know me very well.'

'I know, I know,' he says, leaning back in his chair, looking wistful and heartbreakingly sincere. 'And I'm sorry for thinking you were.'

God damn his civility. It's going to fuck up everything. This requires a change in game strategy. 'That's not what I meant at all. I'm exactly that sort of girl. Have some more wine.'

By the time we leave the bodega, it's dark. Above the rooftops, the cathedral's tower hovers, luminous and ancient. The orange trees weep scent into the thick evening heat. By an old stone bench, I make him kiss me, raking my fingers through the bristle of his crew cut, pressing my hips against his.

He's hard. The cock tents his trousers. 'Oh, my Lord.' His southern drawl pulls at the words like taffy. 'You *are* that kind of girl.'

To the left of the line of blind men, a window box full of scarlet geraniums lift their hydra heads towards the sun, which has only now crested the tile roof of the house opposite and begun its inexorable descent to the cobbles. Two streets away, the seagulls at the port tear into the azure sky with serrated cries.

'Of course I am. Come on.'

Clutching his sweaty hand, we hurry through the winding, dusty streets, headed for the place I'll perform my small moment of magic.

The alley is still cobbled and dead-ended. This is the place: I read it in three different accounts of the execution. The space remembers, the walls remember. If the old window is shuttered against the dark, that doesn't mean it has forgotten. Tonight there is no sun to ride the wall down to the street, but there are still crimson geraniums in the window box beside the pockmarked plaster. The street may have changed its name, but that can't wipe away the cruelty or heal its past. Only I can do that. Me and this soldier.

'Here,' I whisper, pressing my back into the masonry of memory.

'Are you sure?'

'Of course I'm sure. Right here.'

The finality of bullets sliding into their firing chambers calls the prisoners' minds back into their bodies. Although the Captain will use his service pistol to make the job go faster, there are not enough soldiers to shoot all the prisoners in a single volley.

It's not my words that convince him to overcome his hesitation; it's my hands, deftly popping the first button on his pants. Then the second, and the third, as he kisses me again. My hair catches and snags on the wounded stone.

His hands are up and under my skirt. Feeling the dampness, he tugs at my panties until the thick of my thighs no longer holds them up and they drop to a puddle at my feet.

The four who die first are the lucky ones. Unfortunately, young Arturo is not among them. He begins to scream.

That first sweet finger splits me, teasing, and I know the incantation begins. Not with my words, but with my body. No longer just a sequence of events, I am caught in the roll of the spell. My hips are shameless and so are my hands. They push his jeans and boxers down his hips. His freed cock twitches into the curl of my fingers. I must have it inside me.

For a moment, I wonder how I'm going to engineer the rest of this. I've thought it through so many times, but I haven't actually done it before. I'm a neophyte.

Jim, it seems, has. He guides my arms up to his shoulders, takes a firm grip on my ass cheeks and hoists me up and onto his cock in one surprisingly graceful move. It isn't until he encounters resistance that he hesitates.

'Good... good god,' he stutters. 'You're a...'

'Just push a little harder.' My throat squeezes tight around the sharp pain. He can't stop now. He just can't. I've saved myself for this moment. I've read the histories. I've wept over the stupid, hateful cruelty. I've devised this incantation all on my own to ensure it never happens again. Not here. Not anywhere. It's the smallest of sacrifices, but I know it will work.

'Please,' I say. 'You'll ruin everything.'

Tender as anyone could hope for, he presses his fore-head against the old wall and whispers in my ear, 'Are you sure?'

'Oh, for fuck's sake,' says the Captain, waiting for the soldiers to reload the chambers of their ancient rifles. 'How many times do I have to tell you? Always shoot the noisy ones first.'

I don't answer him. With an almighty tug, I pull myself up by my arms and let myself drop, forcing the head of his cock past my hymen. The back of my blouse rips against the wall. There's no more pain or hesitation. The night dissolves into muscle and sinew and everything is simple and right with the world. His urgent, earnest breath is against my cheek, so full of wanting to be alive. Holding him tight, tucking my face into the crook of his neck, I can feel his pulse. Every thrust pushes away the murderousness of the place, punches holes in the timeline, and scrambles its continuity. He bruises my bones with his body.

When he's finished, he lowers me onto my feet and pulls my bunched up skirt down over my hips. But there's one last thing I need to do to make the spell complete.

I reach between my legs and slide my fingers through the mixture of liquids. Turning, I smear it over the wall and whisper secret words.

The second volley does the job. There are seven fresh splashes of crimson against the ancient wall. Silence returns to the alley only temporarily, before the Velasco *and the* Alboran Sea *begin their bombardment of the city from the port.*

The marine tilts his head. His face is all new, smooth planes in the slanting lamplight.

'What the hell are you doing, babe?'

THE SEA AND THE SHORE

By Tom Watts

That same evening she sat drinking with three young and pretty Israeli girls – barely nineteen, comfortable in their short summer dresses and bikinis, destined for Gaza incursions and dusty, olive drab uniforms – she first saw the boy haul a fish out of a small blue boat and cook it right there on the beach.

Esther was on a two-month trip around the Thai islands, falling in love with the warm sea and the measured unbuckling of responsibilities. She was travelling alone, expensively divorced – in her favour – and unable to shake the feeling that she was too old to be drinking Mai Tais with a boat boy. Especially one who's English was practically unintelligible and seemed to get younger after every drink. He had seen her watching him cook the white snapper and offered her a piece, hands out, jerking his fists towards his mouth.

She accepted the food, marvelling at its simple flavour. At home when she cooked fish, she drowned it in white wine or lemon until it tasted like something to be hidden, like a blemish under makeup.

The night passed in a beach bar under a huge tree dressed like a circus, hung with so many lights that if you moved your head too fast it was like falling into a jewellery box. They made passable attempts at conversation, using hand gestures, drawings in the sand and, when they laughed at something one or the other had done, the childish faces of ogres, their fingers pulling cheeks away from gums or widening their eyes until the edges of the sockets were revealed.

'You crazy, lady,' he said, as she laughed at his attempts to draw a small dog in the sand.

'No, You're crazy. I'm Esther.' She pointed at him then herself, giggling at the silly joke. 'And you can't draw dogs.'

'My dog,' he said, pointing at his picture.

'You can keep him. He has three legs.'

'No. This drawing has three legs. He has four in life.'

It was a magnificent night and she felt newly excited about her trip. When she finally went to bed she lay on her back for a while, smiling through the net at the mosquitoes attempting to get to her and listening to the sea drown out the distant beach bar's still-loud music.

Esther's hotel was on a beach the other side of the island from the main town and ferry port. The only way into town was down a dirt track so pitted and distorted by the monsoon rains that the hotel's 4x4 vehicle could manage no more than a sedate mile-an-hour pace. Esther sat in the back of the pick-up and lurched along, sunglasses reflecting the leaf-broken sun. They travelled so slowly she had time to look into every clearing in the jungle; at families of pigs; tiny shacks surrounded by chickens left free to roam, as if they didn't believe in fences; villages clinging to the river, which broke off into smaller and smaller tributaries like slices of lung viewed on a slide. Craggy outcrops lurched from the flatlands like ghost ships, their rigging moss, vines and falling tendrils making almost-shapes that loomed out of the foliage as they drove past. All the while Esther sat, slowly making progress, as if on a ponderous elephant, moving further away from the hotel and closer to the town.

The local town had the feel of a border at the edge of two dangerous countries. Men tried to roughly coax her into shops and restaurants and she saw a child sitting in a pile of rubbish. She ate in a tavern with a crowded pool table and a one-eyed cat sitting on the bar. All the hotel drivers were waiting for the next ferry from the mainland and its cargo of tourists; she saw her hotel's driver drinking a coffee and talking to the barman. They had to wait for the next ferry to pick up the new arrivals to be taken back to the hotel on the 4x4. Esther went to the pharmacy for cosmetics and medicines. The young girl behind the counter caught her looking at the condoms. She was daydreaming; the girl had to tap on the glass counter to get her attention. Esther felt hot and prickly and she saw her face was red as she passed the small mirror on the sunglasses rack.

She returned to the hotel, well-stocked. She need not go back into town for a good while. The hotel was cut off, but at least it looked like the reason she had come to Thailand: white sand beaches and hammocks.

The day of her fifty-fifth birthday she woke up early and went swimming in the night-cold sea, leaving her clothes at the water's edge. Even though the night had lowered the temperature, there were warm strips of water criss-crossing the bay. Esther followed them, enjoying the sharp change in the temperature as she left the warmer sections and plunged into a chilly stretch. She swam towards the cliffs on the west side of the bay with submerged rock gardens at their base. Clumsy, her hands like bread, she pushed herself over the edge of vast underwater canyons, smudged gaps in visibility, descending into dimness. The salt stung her mosquito bites, and she watched tiny jellyfish float by; empty bags of luminosity, floating without will, tide-bound and never truly free. As she swam above a large drop, she imagined the water suddenly disappearing, and her body plunging onto the stones below, dashing her brains upon a large flat stone, spreading her memory across its pink surface. She felt suspended above the altar of a great cathedral, floating like a spirit across the ceiling, awed by the dizzying space.

When she went to get dressed there was a small dog sitting on her clothes. It was a sandy coloured thing, shivering in the weak early morning sun. Esther shooed it off her purple wrap and eyed the animal as she dried herself. 'You're a funny little feller,' she said. It stared back at her and continued with its little shiver dance. 'It's not that cold, you silly little donut.'

A Thai voice shouted from the sea and she saw the boat boy pulling his little blue boat onto the beach. He was shouting to the dog. He covered his eyes, shading them from the low sun and called to the dog again. He could obviously see her but was pretending he couldn't. She was puzzled, then realized she was holding the towel up to her chest but not covering her back. The boat boy was holding up a hand to protect her from embarrassment. She left the towel where it was, set her hips.

'Oops, I'm sorry,' she said.

'Don't be sorry, Miss.'

'Is that your dog?'

'Yes.'

'Is he always so shaky?'

'Saki?'

Esther mimed the dog's strange body quiver.

'Aah! *San*. Yes, he is shaky. Look.' He pointed at the emerging sun. 'It's cold.'

She looked down at her towel-covered body, feeling her gaze draw his eyes in that direction. Quickly, they both looked away, him at the sea, she at the sand; he tried to look involved with the boat and she with the picking up of her clothes. They both became engrossed in their own activities and tried not to notice as they went in separate directions, her toward the shore and him towards the sea, and so they didn't say goodbye.

SUCH IS LIFE

By Sandra Williamson

I remember someone holding me up; I wailed into their chest, their jumper muffling the sound. It was like the noises I'd heard paid mourners make in villages in the south of Spain. When I looked up faces stared, and voices asked me what was wrong. My mouth was open but I couldn't speak. I'd heard of people reacting this way, and dismissed it as a trope used to explain something that can't be explained. Now I knew this was the way it really felt.

Córdoba, Argentina, (31.4036° S, 64.1858° W) 20th October 2010

The hostel's private rooms were in a separate building to the main reception, and there was no WiFi. I took my laptop and crossed the road to the main building to Skype with my mother. She'd just come back from the Nuffield hospital in Newcastle-upon-Tyne where she'd had a second operation for breast cancer. During the first operation five years earlier, there'd been a 'medical oversight' and the doctor hadn't removed the entire tumour on her left breast. She'd driven herself to and from the hospital; my father couldn't have because his license had been suspended years earlier.

She was cheerful, and said she was fine. I felt relieved. I'd been in South America since the beginning of September, and depending on Internet access we spoke every few days. I was heading for Villa General Belgrano next: a Bavarian style village outside Córdoba, founded in the 1930s by a group of German immigrants. She said it sounded like I was having a great time, and she and Daddy really enjoyed seeing the pictures I'd sent. I said nothing. She asked if I wanted her to put him on the phone. We always spoke in Catalan, but she switched to English when she asked me, so he would understand. I said no, I didn't have time. I said I was going to be late, even though the bus wasn't leaving for another two hours. I told her I'd speak to him tomorrow.

Carlisle, Cumbria. (54.8962° N, 2.9316° W) 20th October 2010
You got up from the navy leather sofa when the headlights of the Citroën Xantia illuminated the front room windows. You felt a twinge in your chest, and leaned on the armrest to rise. You felt out of breath. You'd been to hospital three times in the past month because of this. They gave you Omeprazole, a proton pump inhibitor used for patients with gastroesophageal reflux disease, and sent you home with a recommendation to drink less and stop wasting NHS re-sources. You couldn't blame the doctors for misinterpreting your symptoms. You'd turned up to casualty drunk several times, so you could see why they'd think you had heartburn.

You sighed and walked towards the front door. You were standing in the doorway to the living room when she walked in. It was already dark outside, and the cold air that followed her made you shiver.

'You all right?'

'I'm fine, Peter. It all went well.'

'Are you sure? You're not going to die, are you?' The twinge in your chest felt tighter. You thought it might be anxiety. She laughed and reassured you. You followed her into the kitchen. She gave you a hug.

'You look tired, Peter.'

'Aye, well...such is life.' You nodded and rubbed your moustache. She told you she would start making something to eat, and she'd call you when it was ready. You nodded again. On your way out of the kitchen, you turned round. 'You're sure you'll be ok?'

'I'm fine, Peter, really.'

'Just asking.' You shrugged and raised your thick hands

in the air like you always did when you were exasperated. You went back into the living room, and sat on the leather sofa; into the dent your body had made over the years. You felt your breathing going up and down, shallow and quick. The remote control was on the waxed oak coffee table, lying on the scratches you'd made by resting your trainers on it every day while she was at work. You reached out towards the remote with your left hand. You could hear her talking in Catalan to someone on the phone. She always spoke louder when she spoke in Catalan. Not that you understood anything she was saying, anyway.

Your fingers touched the side of the remote control. The twinge in your chest was there again. Your breath got shorter. You tried to open your mouth, and you heard a gasping. Surely that gasping came from somewhere else. The twinge took over, and spread across your chest. You were on the floor now. You tried to call out to her; a gruff wheeze. You could see a crumb of food nestled in the navy carpet pile. The battery cover on the remote had fallen off when you fell to the floor. Your final thought was: now you knew how it felt to die.

Carlisle, Cumbria. (54.8962° N, 2.9316° W) 21st of October 2010
She remembered his face had a dull grey sheen for days. It was like he'd known something was going to happen to him, the same way animals sense storms before they come. When she heard him gasping she left her cousin on the phone and went into the living room. She found him on the floor. 'Oh, Jesus!' she said. It was more a cry for help than an exclamation. She ran back to the phone, and told her cousin that he'd collapsed and she had to call an ambulance. Her thin fingers pressed the nine key, three times. She pulled the phone into the living room, and tried to follow the instructions the man sitting in a call centre gave her but he'd been too heavy for her to move into the recovery position. She would come to obsess about this and feel guilty.

The ambulance crew arrived within minutes, but she could have sworn they'd taken hours. They tried to resuscitate him using a defibrillator. She doubled over the staircase, pleading with God.

The ambulance crew pronounced him dead, there.

They put him onto a stretcher. Curious neighbours stood on their doorsteps, hands over their mouths as he was carried out to the ambulance. She drove to the hospital behind them in her own car. Later, she phoned his mother, but his brother said it was better to come in the morning. There was nothing they could do now.

She slept alone in the house.

Mendoza, Argentina (32.8905° S, 68.8420° W) 21st of October 2010

That night I spent thirteen hours on a bus from Córdoba to Mendoza. During the journey, I misplaced a blue peanut M&M and subsequently found it nestled in my belly button. When I arrived at the Empedrado hostel, I checked in and signed up to go on a bicycle tour of the wineries of Mendoza.

I unloaded my backpack in my room. The bathroom light wasn't working, so I showered in the dark. Sitting on the bed, my hair still damp, I checked my e-mails. I found a message from my sister telling me to phone home immediately, it was not a joke, I had to phone right now, she said.

The Internet connection in the room was weak. I panicked. I thought something was wrong with my mother. I remember the springtime sun, shining on the white tiles in the corridor as I walked into the common dining area.

I sat at a battered picnic table and called my sister. I asked her what the matter was.

She told me Daddy was dead.

SLEEPLESS

By Bill Carey

The first thing he noticed was the way she tilted her head when she posed for pictures. She was at a movie theatre and a fan spotted her and started a conversation, and he stepped into the background as she chatted.

No, she answered a familiar question with a high-pitched laugh, rolling her eyes and smiling, *of course I'm not here to see my own film. Goodness, no. Just wanted to see how a real actress does it.* Then she giggled in a way that made her seem younger than twenty-two.

Eventually, the fan asked for a picture. She smiled and, at the last moment, tilted her head to the left. He found it strange. Why did she always do that? But he decided it was just one of her quirks, and he grew to appreciate it.

In interviews, she claimed she hated the loss of privacy that came with fame. She wanted to be a regular person, she said. *I just don't want people in my business.* He didn't believe it. In the beginning, she'd seemed to avoid him. But he could feel across a room, that she was acting for him. She was quite good, like in her films. She pretended he didn't exist but from the way she smiled into the distance as she twirled her hair or spoke just loud enough for him to hear, he knew it was an act.

Was she just using him for attention? He hadn't been sure. She didn't need it. All she needed to do was leave her security for a few hours, and she'd get more attention than she could handle. She wouldn't want her fans to know, but she left her bodyguards behind twice a week: on Sundays, when she went to service, and on Wednesdays, when she snuck off to some small bookstore in whatever city she was in that week.

She had a favourite place in every city, but she occasion-
ally ventured away from them. He didn't like it when she
surprised him, picking some unfamiliar place, but he understood that she couldn't get into a routine. She needed new
events to energize her, and he was happy to oblige. Besides
the fame, the travel was what she liked least about her pro-
fession. She slept in seven cities some weeks. She didn't
seem to realize that all the activity wore down the people
closest to her.

She usually wore a sweatshirt on her bookstore journeys, pulling up the hood if it rained or she wandered into a
crowded area. She loved poring over anything old. Often,
she asked the proprietor to see the oldest book in the store.
In the US, she would typically get something from the 1600s
and she would sit, studying the cover and the binding, feeling the worn edges with her fingers, flipping through a few
pages. Then she would close the book and study the cover
some more, turning it over and holding it up to the light,
examining every external detail, before handing it back to
the owner and looking around the store.

She took her time. She admired eighteenth-century
maps on the walls and first editions of F. Scott Fitzgerald
books on the shelves. Finally, with a dramatic wave of her
arm, she would reach toward the book she wanted. She
loved colonial diaries, but bought detective novels. He
laughed once when she thought she'd discovered a hidden
gem, *The Maltese Falcon* by Dashiell Hammett. He laughed
too hard, it seemed, because she and the owner glared at
him for a moment. He apologized. She smiled, and he knew
she forgave him.

She always forgave. She wasn't a diva. He had been close
with another actress for a time, and that actress caused a
scene if someone upset her. He had been on the wrong end
of her rage more than once. When their relationship ended,
that actress sent one of her lackeys, an uneducated body-

guard, to tell him they were done.

She wasn't like that. Every once in a while, she ditched her guards for an extra day out – a movie in a small town theatre or a walk through a shopping mall in a middle-class suburb. He liked her best when she did that. She seemed most real, most exposed. Nothing energized her more. She laughed at the small things. At a mall once, he heard her giggle as a teenager jumped on his friend's back and started yelling, *I'm a cowboy! Carry me, horsey, carry me! I wanna ride!*

She was always dignified. He could tell by her mannerisms – and those of the people she was talking to – that she treated people like they were equals. She made eye contact and nodded her head when they spoke. When they said she must feel out of place in a movie theater with turquoise floor tiles and '90s arcade games, she laughed and said it was nicer than the theatre in her hometown.

The first time he saw her at a theatre, he thought it was an act: the movie star pretending to be a regular person. When a fan approached, she smiled wide, her dimples making her look five years younger, her brown hair a mess, and chatted happily about whichever one of her dozen films was this person's favourite. *Of course*, she exclaimed, *that was my favourite, too. I really connected with that character.* Since that time, he'd noticed it never seemed to matter which character they were talking about.

But he'd learned her smile was sincere. She wanted to interact with real people, even if they were fans. They were her driving force. She was holding onto her identity: the teenager from rural Montana who had been discovered on a family vacation, starred in a television ad for peanut butter and shone so brightly the opportunities kept coming. She could reach another level of emotion in her acting. You didn't just understand why her character was crying. You were crying, because there was no other way to feel.

That ability made her a star, but she didn't act like one.

She was just another person at the movie theatre. If people happened to stare because she was famous and beautiful, so be it. She always made sure to ask the fans a question or two. What were they seeing? What snacks were they getting? Anything to keep the conversation going.

She loved the little girls the best. She talked to them for as long as she could. She always asked about school. *Do you get good grades?* she said. They usually said, yes they did. *Good*, she said, *it's good to be smart*. The girls usually said something like, *You're so pretty. When I grow up, I want to be a movie star just like you.*

She smiled and sometimes sighed and said thank you. She always told them they were pretty, too, but it was better to be smart. The first few times he heard her say that, he had been impressed. Maybe she was acting, but the message seemed on point. He wasn't standing close enough, though. Once, he thought she was moving on and started to follow her to the theatre. But she stopped and tapped the little blonde girl on the shoulder. Far enough so the girl's mother couldn't hear, she whispered, *Being pretty's not too bad, either*, and gave her a wink. The girl smiled a goofy smile, a gap between her front teeth, and ran after her mom.

If she could, she would sit and talk all day. She was great at small talk, but he could sense in her a desire to get deeper. Of course, the irony was that she had to answer far more questions than she got to ask. For every movie, she ran the circuit of late-night talk shows, and schmoozed on couches and tried to act natural. But no conversation could be real with a commercial agenda. *By the way, I'm in a movie and here's a clip.*

He disliked the media gauntlet. For one, he couldn't be with her as much as he wanted. Nothing was as emasculating as watching her on television because they couldn't make room for him. Even when he sat in the audience, it wasn't the same. There were too many other people around. Sometimes, she didn't even seem to notice him. He knew that was just the pressure of doing her job. He understood.

The time he liked her least, though, was when she walked the red carpet for premieres and awards shows. It wasn't her fault. It was them. He hated the way the people yelled at her.

He hated the way the paparazzi swooped in, waiting for any mistake they could sell – an ugly dress, a funny face, a low-cut top. They told her to keep her head still. *Don't tilt it so much.* Once, he was taking a shortcut through an alley as she snuck out the back of a club following an awards show after-party. He spotted a photographer hiding behind a garbage can, secretly snapping. After she drove away, he put the photographer in a chokehold and held him until he passed out. Then he smashed the man's camera. Pieces of glass fell to the ground. He caught his finger on a jagged edge of the broken lens. He wiped the blood on the front of his jeans. The shattered glass crunched beneath his feet as he walked away.

Mostly, he hated the way people praised her. Interviewers always complimenting her with fake words, other stars throwing fake love in her direction. *She's an amazing talent, but an even better person. I'm so blessed to work with her. I hope we stay friends.* They didn't even know her. He knew her. He went everywhere with her.

One day, at a movie theatre or shopping mall or maybe one of those small bookstores, when her security wasn't there, he would finally speak to her. He would tell her all he knew about her, and she would recognize it was true: he loved her, and she loved him, too.

THE LEXICO PROJECT
By Michael Zand

The objective of The Lexico Project is to try to make sense of topical, in-teresting or ambiguous phrases by engaging with foreign languages through a procedure called the lexico-positional method. The procedure works like this:

Step 1: a topical, interesting or ambiguous phrase is selected
Step 2: the key nouns in that phrase are located in an English dictionary
Step 3. the dimensional position of those words are calculated as ratios of the total dimensions of the dictionary
Step 4: using dictionaries of the top 20 official languages of the world, the same positions are found and the corresponding words in these positions are noted
Step 5: these new words are assigned appropriate prepositions and listed in rank order by size of official language population

> *war on terror*
> *english* war on terror
> *mandarin* cladding of envy
> *hindi* collusion with crows
> *spanish* prostitution of tenure
> *russian* chaos of indulgence
> *french* removal of command
> *arabic* enshrinement of race
> *portuguese* geysers on reptiles
> *malay* students of carrots
> *bengali* convection by heatstroke
> *japanese* standardisation by universities
> *german* largesse on roller-skates

urdu enunciation of poetry
italian mendacity of interplay
korean science on fire
vietnamese search for colour
persian postponement of injustice
tagalog ritualism of mouthpieces
thai consolidation of boots
turkish decay for personal gain

quality of life
english quality of life
mandarin formulation of romance
hindi honour of illness
spanish contest of giving
russian treatment of sacrifice
french exposure of purpose
arabic hypothesis of doubt
portuguese rendition on falsehood
malay project of spite
bengali bubble of unity
japanese emulation of welcomes
german malfunction of smoke
urdu plague of dreams
italian reflection of hurt
korean suspension of metaphor
vietnamese framework of entertainment
persian illustration of robots
tagalog accordance of materials
thai employment of type
turkish purchase of depression

the new generation of poets
english the new generation of poets
mandarin the new archivers of continentals
hindi the new hairdressers of cuckoos
spanish the new photocopiers of benefits

russian the new employers of pop
french the new heroes of acronyms
arabic the new brains of boredom
portuguese the new wrecking of understanding
malay the new victims of dependence
bengali the new fans of central heating
japanese the new players of weekly magazines
german the new expressways to aesthetics
urdu the new reactionaries to prescriptions
italian the new elevators of fear
korean the new courage of hypocrisy
vietnamese the new calculators of contact lenses
persian the new merchants of bull
tagalog the new soul of telephone directories
thai the new critics of the ordinary
turkish the new culture of no

THE RABBIT

By Jo Schinas

I leant out over the rail as the ferry chugged into the bay. We always came from Madrid to La Manga, on the seaside, for our summer holiday; but Mamá and Papá hadn't taken us to the nearby island before, though my sister and I nagged to visit it every time. Esperanza, who was smaller and who stood behind me, had to lean out even farther than me to see. Our mother took hold of the backs of our sundresses.

We stepped off the ferry into the throbbing of cicadas. Other tourists littered the sand, slouching round iceboxes, sunbathing. Mamá and Papá settled down with a cooler of beers. Esperanza and I played on the shore for a while, searching for the shells with the prettiest pastel insides, and then we decided to explore the slopes behind the beach.

The cicadas' noise got bigger as we climbed the red hillside, barefoot. We soon stuck our flip-flops back on, for there were devil's thorns in the dust. Now that we'd left the shoreline and the wind was gone, we felt the full force of the heat. It had split the patches of mud into splinters. We could smell it too: we smelt drought, smelt ochre. I came across a bird's skull lying on some pebbles. It was as warm as the stones, and as clean, and I thought it a lovely little object. I followed its contours with a finger. I couldn't take it with me, since my dress had no pockets. I'd have liked it as a souvenir.

Higher up the slope we found the rabbit. I spotted it first. I halted on the track; then Esperanza stopped behind me as she saw it too. It hung in one of the thorn-bushes, hooked by a back leg. I suppose it had snagged itself as it leapt. I don't know how long it had been dangling there. It began to jerk its body as we stepped towards it, trapping its foot tighter in the fork. We snapped the branches easily; they were brittle, like bones. The rabbit tried to run as it flopped into the dirt, but its leg was dragging behind it. I lifted the creature, feeling it shudder as my hands closed round it, and cuddled it to my chest. So light, so breakable, as starved as these hillsides, its sides flinching rhythmically against me.

'Shhh...' I said. I stroked its back, the sweat from my palms making its fur streaky.

We hurried to ask our parents what to do. We hoped they'd let us look after the rabbit, perhaps train it as our pet. We talked over one another: each of us wanted to tell the story. The animal, further frightened, scrabbled at me.

'Can we keep it?' I said. 'Please can we keep it?'

'Please, please, please!' said Esperanza.

Our parents chuckled a little. They looked at each other, preparing to reply, and I knew we hadn't a chance.

'You're not bringing it with you,' said Mamá. 'You'd never tame it anyway. Don't be silly.'

I looked at the rabbit. It didn't doubt that I'd kill it. Its eyes, dilated into black, didn't plead with me.

'Leave it in some shade,' said Papá.

Esperanza and I climbed the slope a second time. Though the sun's heat blurred the distance, its light sharpened all that was nearby. The shadows, like their bushes, were skeletons. They wouldn't be much shelter from the sky. The edges of those shadows could have cut me; serrated lines here, straight lines there.

We found some shade slightly denser than the rest. When I set the rabbit down, it didn't move. It looked too weak. Its eyes were still wide. Esperanza had a sandwich from the picnic; she set it down beside the creature.

'It'll want food while it's getting better,' she said.

We left the rabbit huddled on the hillside. We returned to the rest of the tourists, down on the shore.

THE TROUBLE WITH
PARALLEL UNIVERSES
By Peter Benney

I

A stack of books, a cup of Earl Grey and a newspaper cover the desk in Thomas Miller's study. It is Sunday afternoon and Thomas, who calls himself a freelance essayist, is too tired to continue research for his latest work, 'The Detailed History of the Public Toilet'. He sips his tea, folds his paper and closes his eyes.

This will probably be the last essay he writes. Thomas is thirty-three and technically unemployed, and if he cannot sell this essay he will give up and get a job in an IT department instead. Thomas does not want a job in an IT department but he can't do much else besides that and writing essays. He is living off the money from his previous essay, a study of 'The Lasting Effects of Rollercoaster Nausea'. It sold to a small journal for a modest price, and met with adequate critical praise. It paid his bills and stocked his cupboards. His girlfriend is a patient woman.

Thomas opens his eyes and sits up when he hears Claudia come upstairs. He pokes his head out of the office.

'You okay?' he asks her.

'Yeah. Come and watch telly with me, love. You're working too hard. It's Sunday.'

'I know. I'm thinking. I'll be down in a bit.'

'Alright, but if you stay here thinking all afternoon, I'll

have to come and take you by force!' Claudia bends down and kisses him before heading downstairs. She shuts the office door behind her. She and Thomas have been together for three years.

Thomas looks out of the window, beyond his reflection, beyond the park below and into the rest of the world. Life could be worse. It could be better, too, but he has Claudia, his home, and his health. Sometimes he tries to imagine his life with someone else, somewhere else, and sometimes it appeals.

He turns off his computer, leans back in his chair and sleeps. He dreams about meeting the inventor of the urinal cake. I've got a question for you, Thomas says. Why did you call it a cake?

II

A stack of books, a cup of Earl Grey, and one Thomas Miller. He's taken the afternoon off to work through a backlog of Sudoku and *Guardian* crosswords. The logic puzzles are a welcome change from his latest essay that explores the theoretical possibility of 'Words that Rhyme with Orange and their Impact on Modern Poetry'.

This will probably be the last essay he writes. He knew it would be a challenge when he came upon the subject, but now he is convinced that this essay will ruin him and he wishes he never started, wishes he could just take back the library books, delete his computer files and pretend it never happened. It is not like Thomas to abandon a project, but this time he might have to break his rule. Three weeks of research and no results. The toddlers in the poetry corner giggled at his questions and the librarians laughed him out of the library. At least his girlfriend is a patient woman.

He hears Claudia come upstairs.

'You okay?' he asks her.

'Not bad. Might be better if you came and kept me company.' She peers over his shoulder at his stack of puzzles. 'You're like a hamster on a wheel. Do you ever stop?'

'I like to keep busy.'

'As if I need reminding. Come and watch the telly with me. Something trashy.'

'Maybe later, love.'

Claudia goes downstairs. Thomas switches on his ancient computer. As the monitor lights up he catches a glimpse of his own face, a digital doppelganger. He pulls up an Internet browser and types in: nine letters, *underskin point*. He spins around in his office chair and works it out before the computer finds any results. *Syringe*. He groans, leans back in his chair and dreams of other words that don't quite rhyme with orange.

III

Books, teacups and Thomas Miller. Typing with the fervour of a thousand academics. Read more journals than Sigmund Freud himself. Thoroughly convinced that this essay will be the one that makes him: 'Five Practical and Applicable Uses for Recycled Beeswax.' Not exactly life changing, for him or anyone else, but scientifically sound, if the *British Medical Journal* is anything to go by. Thomas feels witty, knowledgeable and authoritative. He hammers out the concluding lines of his draft and clicks save three times, to make sure. He hears Claudia come up the stairs.

'You okay?'

'Fine. How's it going?' she asks, noticing his good mood.

'Great. I'm done.'

'Done?'

'First draft. Done for today.'

'Wanna watch *Come Dine With Me*?' Claudia winks at him. Thomas, closet cook, grins. Guilty pleasure TV.

'Go on then. I'll put the kettle on.'

On the living room sofa, Claudia leans back into

Thomas's arms. Her long hair smells of peaches. Before they switch on the TV, Thomas sees their reflections framed within the glass box of the screen. The fake couples on TV have nothing on us, he thinks.

IV

A nest of books scattered and open, books wedged into other books, books folded into larger books, little paperback books used as bookmarks in the library's hardcover books. An industrial-sized mug of room temperature Earl Grey perfumes the stale room. Thomas Miller is exhausted and he hasn't even started. He has been commissioned to write 'Blancmange and Me: The Meaning Behind the Milk' for his favourite gastropub publication. Thomas likes food, including desserts, and blancmange is, well, in his top eight, or nine. But where should he begin? What to say, and why? The empty white page seems to ripple like a dish of the milky pudding, dulling his brain into a stodgy silence.

A voice interrupts his concentrated panic.

'Make me a cuppa!'

Thomas ignores it.

'Come on, babe! I'm gasping.'

Still ignores it.

'Ba-abe? You up there?'

'Coming,' Thomas finally says. He could do with a fresh one too.

Beth is sprawled across the sofa watching trash TV and eating crisps. Beth has been living with Thomas for three months. Thomas wishes he lived alone. She isn't even his girlfriend. They'd had sex a few times, but only for something to do. Now he tries not to touch her. He sits on the armchair.

'You finished that letter yet?' she asks. 'We need to sort out dinner.'

'It's an essay,' Thomas explains once again. 'It's not

really the sort of thing you can finish in one sitting.'

'Not like this tube of Pringles then, ha!' Beth cackles and sprays crumbs. She points the near-empty tube towards her housemate. Nothing but halves and salt. 'You want some?'

V

You want some dinner but you have to start this essay first. You've scouted the journals, assessed the market, chosen your subject and you've got a title. 'Reality v. Real TV: What Essex Really Thinks.' You're mildly interested. You've read up on the subject, compiled your arguments. You've turned on the computer. But now you'd rather read a book, or watch *Doctor Who*, or go out and find some company, someone to bring home in the early hours. You turn around in your swivel chair and knock a mug of tea onto the carpet. Now the room smells like citrus and stale milk. You pick up the mug and leave the stain.

You open up an Internet browser and search for 'cooking jobs'. You feel like you're searching for the intangible. *Chef jobs, cook jobs, London cook jobs, fish4jobs* – something about that one seems promising. *Experience needed.* You turn away.

You find yourself thinking about that girl from halls, your student days. She was a cook. Every night; stews, salads, roasts, pastries. Did she ever study? At least the fridge was never empty. She never used a book, rarely followed a recipe. She crafted meals from the contents of your cupboards. And you can't remember her name. Clara? Claire? She was cook material. She was cute. You'll just have to settle for writing about cooking. What's for dinner? Chips. You're sick of chips.

VI

Thomas isn't working on an essay this week. 'Lasting Effects of Rollercoaster Nausea' was more interesting than he expected (or intended). The *BMJ* wanted to reprint it, and said so in a very polite letter. Page four, big money. He signed a little contract and wrote a polite reply. Got his cheque in the post. Cashed it.

He waited a few days. The cheque cleared. Bank balance went up. And now Thomas is getting commission letters. They want more. One strikes his fancy: 'Porcupine Quills: For Pens or Pills?'

Thinking it over, he heads to the high street. The jeweller is very pleased to hear Thomas's good news. He directs Thomas to the most beautiful rings they have for sale. Thomas picks an elegant one. The price surprises him, but he reminds himself he can afford it now. He pays and hurries home.

She is on the sofa watching trash TV. A presenter with an awful haircut and a cheesy grin. Hardly a romantic moment, but he can't wait. This day has been three years in the making.

He sits down beside her and leans in. Her hair smells like peaches but there's crisp crumbs down her front. He digs into his pocket and pulls out a little box.

'Beth, I've got a question for you.'

VII

'Claudia, I've got a question for you.'

'Shouldn't you be working on, er, what was it again?' She doesn't turn around straight away.

'Er, it's called 'Losing Oneself: A Freudian Approach to Hedge Mazes'. I wanted the one about porcupines but they wouldn't – er, anyway.' Thomas holds his fist out in front of Claudia and opens it. A gummy ring, orange, with a lemon diamond. 'Will you, um, marry me?'

Claudia laughs. 'Yum. I'll have to chew it over.' She eats the gummy. 'A very sweet gesture. I'll need more of these before I'm a kept woman, though. How about trout for dinner? I can pop down the high street. Get some coriander. You okay?'

Thomas realises he must look uneasy, because she looks concerned. 'I know we aren't doing so well, lately, financially, but, er,' he says. That's where Thomas's speech ends. He's distracted by the impossible idea of someone else living his life better than he can. Maybe they should already be married. Maybe he's too slow. He looks at her.

'Shit,' says Claudia. 'You really mean it.'

'Yes. I mean, we won't be living in this dump forever. We can get our own place, and save up for a nice wedding. We've known each other ten years, Claudia. We've waited long enough.'

'Okay. Okay! Yes! Of course I'll marry you.' She smiles and kisses Thomas on the lips. Now he's really got to sell that essay. Now he feels lost.

VIII

Books, teacups, monitor.

'Cuppa! Gasping!'

Crumbs. Beth smells greasy. She works at the chippy on the corner. Thomas sits on the armchair. An advert for a reality programme comes on. Thomas usually makes a point of ignoring advertising in all its forms, but this one grabs him because his own face is plastered on the screen amid an ocean of brightly coloured slogans and pound signs. He sits up and pays attention.

'*You are currently viewing: Money TV! This is you,*' announces the TV. Thomas's face bobs around in time with the music, distorted with whitened teeth and bleach-blond hair. '*And this is what you're worth.*' Thomas is embarrassed to see his own anaemic bank balance broadcast on TV. He stands up, outraged.

'This can't be legal,' he mutters, then again, louder. 'This can't be legal!'

'What do you mean?' says Beth. 'What's wrong? I like this programme.'

'I don't,' he replies, calming down. He sits. 'It's too familiar.'

'It's reality TV, love. It's meant to be realistic. You okay?'

'I'd much rather be working. Or reading a good book.'

'I've got a question for you,' says Beth, but Thomas is already running upstairs, ignoring her. He switches on his computer and pulls up his latest work, 'Do Androids Dream of Electric Books? Debunking the eReader Gimmick'. He shudders. Thomas fears for a world without proper books.

IX

Thomas screams and lurches forwards, out of his chair and onto the floor. His fall is cushioned by a stack of old newspapers, from which he has yet to cut out the Sudokus. He hears footsteps charging up the stairs.

'You okay?'

'Fine, I think. Just a funny dream. Thanks, love.'

'You're working too hard. You're –'

'Like a hamster, yeah. I know. But what about you? Meeting the defendant on a Sunday?' Thomas stands up and frowns. 'You won't acquit anyone with ketchup on your tie, Clark.' Thomas unties it, goes into the bedroom and picks Clark another. The one with the crossword pattern. He always looks good in that one.

'Thanks,' says Clark. They kiss. 'I'll see you later, Tommy.'

'See you.' Thomas sits down and considers a new essay title: 'Mealtime is Cochineal Time: Five Food Dyes to Die For'. Before he can commit it to the page, the subject triggers a vivid burst of memory. His best friend from halls, Claudia. A phenomenal cook. She fed the entire floor. Only ever bought organic, so her complexion was flawless. For her, ketchup was practically an illicit substance. And she really liked him. He just didn't have the heart to break it to her.

X

Crumbs. Adverts. Armchair. Thomas drums his fingers excitedly on the arms and stretches his feet. He is surprised yet pleased to see his own face on TV, in a living room exactly like his own. He always knew he would do well, just not like this.

'I hate this programme,' says Beth. She reaches for the remote.

'Leave it on,' says Thomas, holding up his hand. 'Give it a minute. Let's see what happens.'

TV-Thomas is curled up with a woman Thomas recognises but could not name. They're talking but the conversation is muted.

'She's gorgeous,' says Thomas out loud. 'They're doing you a favour.'

Beth scoffs.

TV-Thomas reaches into his pocket and pulls out a little box. He flips the lid open.

The woman laughs, hugs TV-Thomas, kisses him. Happy ending. Thomas feels like he's watching a biopic and a documentary at once.

'I don't get it,' says Beth. 'Why's there no sound?'

'You okay?' Thomas's question goes unanswered as TV-Thomas stands up and walks towards the camera. He taps on the lens with his knuckles and the audio track comes on. *Dink dink.*

'*I'm you,*' says TV-Thomas loudly and clearly. '*I'm you! I'm telling you. Whatever you're thinking, or feeling, it's true, it's all true, and -'*

Thomas turns and looks at Beth, who is dusted with crumbs, and pointing the remote at the TV.

XI

Thomas downs the last of his tea, slams his book shut and turns off the monitor. He charges downstairs and points wildly at the TV.

'The news,' he says. 'Put the news on!'

'What's going on?' asks Claudia, annotating one of her own recipes with a biro.

'Just put it on!'

She changes the channel and a newsreader shuffles papers. As she announces the next story Thomas throws himself onto the sofa beside her.

'Have you experienced extreme dizziness or sickness for prolonged periods after riding on the famed Terror Twister? How about the Serpent's Spiral?' The newsreader smiles. Beside her, the co-host shakes his head.

'You'd never get me on one of those.'

'Me neither, because new research suggests that the G-forces exhibited by these exciting attractions can actually result in a variety of illnesses and conditions previously thought to be unconnected. New research conducted and published by *British Medical Journal* researcher Dr. Thomas Miller –'

Claudia's scream drowns out the rest of the report. 'You're famous!'

'Hardly,' Thomas replies, through his laughter.

'You will be!'

'Maybe.'

Claudia pauses. 'I thought that essay bombed...'

'Me too.'

She shrugs and wraps her arms around him. Thomas allows himself to relax. Perhaps this is the essay that makes him. 'It's not over, though. I'm planning a follow-up study. 'Going Nowhere Fast: The Sociological Implications of Merry-Go-Rounds'.' Thomas reaches into his pocket. 'And I've got a question to ask you.'

Claudia points. 'Hey. That newsreader. Don't you recognise him?'

Thomas shakes his head.

'It's Clark. Remember Clark?'

'He always was a smug bastard.'

XII

Thomas rests his head on the keyboard and shuts his eyes. His work-in-progress, titled 'Six of Me and Half a Dozen of You: The Trouble with Parallel Universes', has been interrupted by the phone ringing. He listens to Claudia's muffled voice coming from downstairs, the highs and lows, the questions and answers.

He hears her coming up the stairs. She looks manic.

'You okay?'

'You'll never guess who that was,' she says. 'Go on.'

'Well if I'll never gu-'

'It was Clark. Clark from halls. You remember him, right?'

'Unfortunately.' Thomas remembers his patronising tone of voice, his flawless grades, his immaculate dress sense and his insufferable good luck.

'He wants a catch-up.' Thomas braces himself and listens. 'He's made it big on the stock markets and is investing in some IT firm!' There it is. Clark never missed an opportunity to gloat. Smug bastard. 'I always knew he'd do well. He's invited me over for dinner tomorrow night. You never know. He might be in the market for a wife. He's the majority shareholder now, so I could do much worse!' She giggles and walks away. 'I'm going to make him a cheesecake,' she thinks out loud.

'Lovely.' Why do they call it a cake, he wonders as she walks off. He is about to rest his head on the keyboard again when a notification pops up. An email. It appears he has sent it to himself.

XIII

From: tjmiller1979@gmail.co.uk (Thomas Miller)
Sent: 25 November 2012 16:07
To: tjmiller1979@gmail.co.uk (Thomas Miller)
Subject: Six of Me and Half a Dozen of You
Attachments: The Trouble with Parallel Universes.doc
(29 KB)[Open as Web Page]

Thomas,
I know it looks like you've sent this email yourself. And technically, you have. But the fact that you don't remember writing it should be enough reason to keep reading.

You've been having doubts lately; about your work, your relationships, the trajectory of your life. You feel like you're simultaneously far more successful and far less successful than you ever thought possible. (And I feel as though I truly am writing to myself because I've experienced these same doubts.) I've sent these emails in all directions in the hope of reassuring myself infinite times over that somewhere, I'm doing okay. I hope I get to read them every time. I've even received some myself.

It was Asimov who posited that an infinite number of universes meant an infinite number of different outcomes from each universe $\infty2$. This means infinite universes where I am unemployed, infinite universes where you are married. Infinite lifetimes alone. Infinite lives with infinite lovers. I imagine it like a Sudoku puzzle, every universe containing essentially the same information, but each time arranged differently. I suppose this means there's a chance you never met Claudia.

I should also ask you not to try and respond to this email, because we have the same email address and you will fail, but there is infinite chance that you are as capable of contacting me as I am you. I will look forward to your reply. As for me, this email is the culmination of decades of research, not all of which was my own. As you read this you conclusively prove the existence of parallel universes. (Are you a physicist too?) In any case, your universe may never have nurtured this technology, so it is best left unexplained. I dread to think what disasters may occur thanks to my interference.

I have attached one piece of proof. In a mind-bending encounter with another Thomas Miller, I discovered he had already written extensively on the possible existence of alternate realities. Beaten me to it, I suppose. I read some of this work. Fiction, or fact? Either way it feels eerily familiar. See attachment.

And what else of my life? I am a physicist, yes, and I'm doing well for myself. I expect 'Six of Me and Half a Dozen of You', the paper accompanying my research, will be my last. My work in the field will make me rich enough to retire. I have been in love with Claudia for ten years. We are never apart. We are happy and I am going to propose soon. You may hear from me again.

Thomas Miller

Thomas sips his tea and scrolls to the top of the email.

Attachments: The Trouble with Parallel Universes.doc (29 KB)
[Open as Web Page]
　　Thomas clicks, reads.
　　You are currently viewing: The Trouble with Parallel Universes.doc (29 KB)

WRITE CLUB

By Katie Seth

We've seen the best lines of our work destroyed by red ink, colourful fountain pens, scrawling their way across the nervous sheets on Wednesday afternoons, looking for things to fix.

Sleepyheaded writers double spacing for others to scribble in margins, track changes and suggest rephrasing at stupid times in the night.

Like this is the most dull opening imaginable! I am immediately intrigued and obviously the roar is distant if it is in the distance.

Like ADVERB and Heidi needs to get over clichés and foreshadow this and unclear to new readers or do you want a semicolon?

Like will teenagers understand this and how will it influence their behaviour? Subtle, as microfiction should be. Do they shamble or run?

Like give me more details. And do you want to start sentence with 'and'? I'm drawn in now so pick one, you can't have both, and here, have a semicolon.

Like overpoweringly all this equals really good, love this tension, clarify otherwise funny and Crikey he's keen!

Like 'She' or 'been' and fuzzily according to Peter the first three pages are quite confusing and ADVERB.

Like how about a semicolon here? They are perfect because they can break skin. You sound like a weirdo and I'm almost certain they have something against the word 'whilst'.

Like this doesn't follow on from the previous sentence,

is this real? You should have capital letters, because that's just a script.

Like my head has been frazzled today and it sounds a little CLICHÉ for some reason. It seems too negative.

Like consider cutting. Emo. I don't understand but consider cutting. Then it will make sense. Would you like to use a semicolon?

Like a bit melodramatic and this does not seem appropriate and adverbs can be easily lost but girls like cartoons, right?

Like when Lucy needs to prolong the mystery of his secret a little longer but I didn't realise the library rented out toilet rolls.

And it could be an idea to murder that darling and you pulled off the killing and make more obvious, make less obvious, a bit too obvious.

Like Kadeem's time jumps aren't working and please excuse the gamma and punction, I preferred this when it was described.

Like you state the obvious a lot and the reader is also surprised. Perhaps lose the specificity on the final sandwiches.

Like insert coma and that's two out of five and do you need the capital letters? Really? Fix sentence and don't gloss over it and you can have a semicolon if you want one.

The wound began to what?!?! No line break. All you need is snot but since you're fantasy you're fine and balance backstory.

Like must she shriek? You've not set her up as a football fan and you really should have a semicolon and murder your darling with it.

Like CLICHÉ and CLICHÉ and ADVERB and CLICHÉ and I miss the sentence you've taken out. I thought it was funny and the thing in the car.

Like don't worry about this one anymore missing spaces between words or what effect it has for the story apart from coolness.

Like Jemma is too possessive and take away adverbs with prawn crackers. And so subtle a seagull called Gavin and this image doesn't work.

Like I'm laughing. Am I supposed to be laughing? It feels like an unmurdered darling to me so where is your wider reading list? Is this intentional?

And you are giving away the end a bit and park more detail; epic important place and the only thing that would be an issue was underage sex and that wasn't a challenge.

Like nice is a little too pathetic a word for the smell of a guy she has a major crush on and would you like a semi-colon, he seems very arrogant.

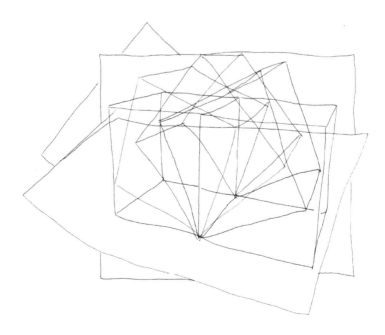

Square Land Once Upon an If (Tamar Levi)

Like this sounds funny and Jess, I love this image and Oooh Mysterious but I don't write sex scenes for people to fall asleep to.

Like lose the commotion; she's not likely to wallow in someone else's and curious word use sounds awkward and ADVERB ADVERB ADVERB, punctuation needed

Or is it right to include OCD? I'm not used to this style of writing, how about a semicolon instead? Narrow it down and zoom in.

Like the bird is talking and leaving us unsatisfied shaking shakily and please take it out; make it not exist, and lose that bit that you had had to add and put that thing back or Anna is going to be way too creepy and get the skewers out and murder your darling.

Like this is unclear and CLICHÉ and she wrinkled her nose and defamiliarise with lovehearts and smiley faces and stretchers and fill Thom's poems with Oxford commas because it's funny.

I see the pattern now, and the characterisation. I don't really care about typos and terrible adjectives and stuff so add a small amount of content from chapters Three and Four to One and Two.

Like hell, I liked it and I didn't care for Howl. Something is very strange about the words "conform" and "innovative" being next to each other.

Like I'll stop moralising and it may actually be redundant altogether but does anyone know if lasagne has a layer of pasta on top?

NOTES ON CONTRIBUTORS

All writers are winners of the annual Creative Writing Day Anthology Competition organised by the Department of English and Creative Writing at the University of Roehampton. The year of competition is indicated in brackets.

Amy Austen [2012] graduated the University of Roehampton in 2012. At the time of publication she works at the travel website mydestination.com, where she writes for a global audience. Austen also writes autobiographical poetry and is planning a book review blog at: about.me/amyausten.

Peter Benney [2013] is an Essex native who wants to emigrate to the moon to write science fiction and fantasy, undisturbed. He gets pleasure from the fact that he shares his birthday with Emily Brontë and Kate Bush. Benney holds a BA in English Literature and Creative Writing. One day he will finish his first novel, *Déja Moo*.

Nanou Blair Gould [2013] writes coming-of-age fiction, short stories, novels, poetry and plays. She believes in active, exciting research to fuel her stories, and in calling herself 'a writer' as an excuse to do it. Blair Gould hopes her stories will inspire readers to do the same.

Bill Carey [2013] is an American journalist who currently works for *Sports Illustrated*. He primarily writes about the intersection of sports and society. Carey spent a year studying at Roehampton on the Fulbright Scholarship's Alistair

Cooke Award in Journalism, reporting on London. He graduated summa cum laude and valedictorian from Northwestern University's Medill School of Journalism in 2012.

JACK CHARTER [2012] lives in Kent. His short stories and poetry have appeared in *Dead Beats* and *Stimulus Respond*. He graduated in 2012 with a BA in Creative Writing from Roehampton. Charter also creates electronic music, and has combined this with poetry from the *Kerosene Chronicle* blog. At the time of publication he is working on a novel and preparing for postgraduate study.

TONI DIPPLE [2012] is the founding director of local food social enterprise, Organic Ilford CIC, and project coordinator of a community mental health project, the Forest Farm Peace Garden. She is a published journalist and a writer of things agricultural and environmental. She is passionate about communicating the unsaid and under-reported. She holds a BA in Creative Writing from Roehampton.

NICHOLAS ELLIOTT [2012] is from Guildford, Surrey. He writes short stories, and poetry and at the time of publication is working on the first draft of a novel. His work centres on themes of love, inspiration and youth culture. Elliott's main passion is cricket and he hopes to eventually work as a sports journalist. He graduated from Roehampton with a BA in Journalism and Creative Writing.

HEDDA ESTENSEN [2012] is a writer and a filmmaker with a background in journalism. She has a BA in Creative Writing from Roehampton and an MA in Digital Film and Television Production. In 2013, Estensen directed her first short film, *Little Spark*. She currently has several scripts in development. Estensen writes fiction, poetry and screenplays; her writing explores psychology and human nature.

AMANDA FRIEZE [2013] is a technical writer and editor at NASA's Jet Propulsion Laboratory in Pasadena, California. She received her MA in Creative and Professional Writing from the University of Roehampton. Her work has appeared in several online journals, including *The Commonline Journal*, *All Things Girl*, and *Emerge Literary Journal*.

HARRY GODWIN [2009] graduated with a Roehampton BA in Creative Writing in 2009. From there, he pursued a career in poetry, founding The Arthur Shilling Press and publishing a number of books. He moved to Devon, started a family and bought some chickens. His current work, *swallows*, will soon be released into the wild.

AUDREY JEAN [2013], a poetry lover, is studying Creative Writing and Film at the time of publication. As a child she wanted to be an astronaut, until she found out writing was another form of space travel. Now, she finds inspiration in philosophy and physical cosmology. As an apprentice filmmaker, she explores the relationship between poetry and the screen.

HALEY JENKINS [2013] is an innovative writer and visual poet. She has two novels-in-progress – *Trusting Pan* and *Bulwark* – and was published in the United Press anthology *In Between the Lines* in 2013. She gets ideas walking around London's South Bank.

HEIDI LARSEN [2013] is a writer and people-watcher who moved to London from Bergen, the rainiest city in Europe. She can be found at her desk in Camden writing short stories, screenplays and poetry. She holds a BA in Creative Writing from Roehampton and is currently studying for an MA in Creative Writing at Birkbeck where she uses her writing to examine human behaviour, societies and dysfunction.

TAMAR LEVI [Illustrations] has spent her life triangulated between desk, bookshelf and easel. Raised in Alaska and now based in Athens, the Cornish-Jewish author and illustrator won the Santander Award for Academic Excellence in 2012 for her PhD in English and Creative Writing at the University of Roehampton. Levi, whose illustrations light up an award-winning book series on philosophy for the primary school classroom, is currently researching a novel and illustrating more books while living with her Greek-Québécois partner and their overflowing window boxes.

MADELEINE MORRIS [2013] is a lecturer and has been writing erotic fiction under the pen name Remittance Girl for over fifteen years. Her short stories appear in a number of anthologies and her novel *Beautiful Losers* is published by Robinson (2012). Madeleine's work focuses on how desire and eroticism construct our sense of self. She is currently pursuing a PhD in Creative Writing at Roehampton. The story included in this collection won the Creative Writing Day Anthology Competition's 'Editor's Choice' Award.

DIANA NORTEY [2009] enjoys losing herself in characters, description and emotion. Nortey writes a monthly online column for *Inspirels Lifestyles*, an inspirational magazine for women. She is motivated by the satisfaction of knowing her readers' needs have been fulfilled. She holds a BA in Creative Writing from the University of Roehampton.

EMILY PARSONS [2013] is an Australian student who ventured to London to study creative writing and philosophy. She's an avid explorer of the natural world and human nature, and aims to map her journeys on the page. She's interested in telling small stories of ordinary people who are searching for meaning in their lives. She hopes to bring attention to her greatest love, Tasmania.

EMMA RIDDELL [2013] completed her Roehampton MA in 2013 and is currently working on the gothic novel *The Other Daughter*. This is a tale in which the Frankenstein myth takes shape in a contemporary family setting, amid concerns about infertility and human cloning. Riddell's aspirations involve sitting on a sofa, dunking digestives, and discussing writing with Sarah Waters. She can be found tweeting on reading, writing and Malkin's current incarnations @EmmaERiddell.

REBECCA ROSIER [2009] is a dancer, copywriter and song-writer based in the South West. Since graduating from Roehampton in 2009, Rosier has worked as a writer in some of London's top advertising agencies; released an electro album as 'Bim' which gained unsolicited press in *The Guardian* and *NME*; and learned to do a headstand.

JO SCHINAS [2013] spent her life travelling until she came to the UK to study. She wrote the first draft of 'The Rabbit' when she fourteen, while resident in the place where the story is set. At the time of publication, Schinas is a third-year Creative Writing student at Roehampton.

KATIE SETH [2013] is a novelist, short story writer and reluctant poet. She has written about vampires, werewolves, turtles and a loaf of bread. Seth holds a BA in Creative Writing from the University of Roehampton. She can be found at katieseth.com.

LEWIS SPRATT [2012] graduated from the University of Roehampton in 2012 with a degree in English Literature and Creative Writing. His writing explores the fantastical elements of everyday relationships, speech, and people. He is fascinated by love's beat, the rhythm of words, and by all our secrets.

EMMA STRAND [2013] is a poet, short story writer and aspiring novelist. Finalist in the Roehampton Creative Writing Day Anthology Competition two years in a row, she experiments with fusions of time-scales and genres. At the time of publication she is writing her first novel.

STEPH VICKERS [2012] is a writer, artist and part-time degenerate. She was born and raised in East London but dreams of living somewhere else. Vickers writes mostly transgressive fiction. She was given the Roehampton Creative Writing Day Anthology Competition's 'Editor's Choice' award for her story, 'Hark The Herald Angel'.

SEAN WAI KEUNG [2013] arranges syllables into poems. He regularly performs his work at poetry slams and performance art festivals. His work was shortlisted for the 2014 Ariadne's Thread Poetry Competition. In 2013, he won a Farrago Zoo Award for Best Debut Performance. He has worked as assistant editor for *Poetry Weekly* magazine and was Roehampton University's Writing Society President 2012-2013. His blog is at waikeungpoetry.wordpress.com.

TOM WATTS [2008, 2009] lives, writes and works in south east London. He calls himself an English teacher, poet and idiot. His newest work, *The Fruit Journal*, was published in 2013 by Knives Forks and Spoons and his eBook/chapbook *The Scavengers of London* is published by Red Ceilings Press. A collection of his blog poetry, *The Fragments*, is available on Amazon. His work has also been published in *Equilibrium Magazine*, *Remark*, *Streetcake Magazine*, *Plus-Que-Parfait*, *zimZalla*, and *La Granada*. His music reviews are published on *Rhum*, an online culture magazine. His websites are chepanzee.com and feedingthebear.blogspot.com. Watts won the Roehampton Creative Writing Day Anthology Competition's 'Editor's Choice' award two years in a row. He holds a first class BA in Creative Writing from Roehampton.

SANDRA WILLIAMSON [2013] is, at the time of publication, a final year undergraduate at Roehampton studying Journalism and Creative Writing. She previously worked as a translator and taught English in several countries. She has a passion for travel and writing about what she sees around her.

LOUISE YOUNG [2012] is a Roehampton BA graduate living in Newcastle. She writes poetry and scripts and works for Open Clasp Theatre Company in Newcastle. Young has just finished her first play and hopes to see it performed somewhere soon, since shows put on in her Mam's living room don't count anymore.

MICHAEL ZAND [2009] is a writer, editor and researcher. His collections include *Kval* (Arthur Shilling, 2009) and *Lion* (Shearsman, 2010). His work was included in the *Best Poetry of 2011* anthology (Salt, 2011). His latest collection *The Wire* was part of the Shearsman series shortlisted for the Michael Marks Award in 2013. He is currently working on a translation of The Rubaiyat of Omar Khayyam entitled *Ruby*. Zand holds a PhD in Creative Writing from the University of Roehampton and teaches on the undergraduate programme.